SUNDAY'S
Word

BISHOP JOHN HEAPS

SUNDAY'S
Word

HOMILIES
FOR
YEAR B

E. J. DWYER

First published in 1996 by
E.J. Dwyer (Australia) Pty Ltd
Unit 13, Perry Park
33 Maddox Street
Alexandria NSW 2015
Australia
Phone: (02) 550-2355
Fax: (02) 519-3218

National Library of Australia
Cataloguing-in-Publication data

    Heaps, John E., 1927–
    Sunday's word: homilies for year B.

    ISBN 0 85574 350 6.

    1. Catholic Church – Sermons. 2. Church year sermons.
    3. Sermons, Australian. I. Title.

    252.6

Cover design by Megan Smith
Text design by Megan Smith
Typeset in Bembo 12/14.5pt by Sun Photoset Pty Ltd, Brisbane
Printed in Australia by Alken Press Pty. Ltd.– Smithfield
10 9 8 7 6 5 4 3 2 1
00 99 98 97 96

Distributed in the United States by:
    Morehouse Publishing
    PO Box 1321
    HARRISBURG PA 17105
    Ph: (800) 877 0012
    Fax: (717) 541 8128

Distributed in Canada by:
    Novalis
    49 Front Street East
    Second Floor
    TORONTO, ONT M5E IB3
    Ph: (800) 387 7164
    Fax: (416) 363 9409

Distributed in Ireland and the U.K. by:
    Columba Book Service
    55A Spruce Avenue
    Stillorgan Industrial Park
    BLACKROCK CO. DUBLIN
    Ph: (01) 294 2556
    Fax: (01) 294 2564

Distributed in New Zealand by:
    Catholic Supplies (NZ) Ltd
    80 Adelaide Road
    WELLINGTON
    Ph: (04) 384 3665
    Fax: (04) 384 3663

There are depths to be fathomed in Christ.
He is like a rich mine with many recesses containing treasures,
and no matter how we try to fathom them,
the end is never reached.
Rather, in each recess, we keep on finding here and there
new veins of new riches.

ST JOHN OF THE CROSS

Please read the Scripture for the Mass of the day.
Then read these homilies.

Where there is no reference given for a quotation, it is from
the readings of the day.

The Gospel references for the readings of each day are
included in the list of contents.

Contents

First Sunday of Advent

"Be on your guard," "stay awake," "stay awake," "stay awake, he must not find you asleep," "stay awake." The same thing is repeated six times in four sentences. It is not a school teacher on Friday afternoon or a parent worried that a child may go to sleep on a train and miss the station. It is Jesus speaking. It is the Word of God. On the other hand, perhaps it is a worried parent—worried that his children will miss the point of life.

These are the final few verses of chapter thirteen of Mark's Gospel. In that chapter Jesus speaks of the end of time, how we can be led astray by false teachers, and of the coming of the Son of Man with power and glory.

In this context and in the context of Isaiah's message today, "Why, Lord, leave us to stray from your ways …?" and "Oh, that you would tear the heavens open and come down," the Church puts to us this appeal of Jesus for our attention.

Be attentive to the things that matter: the Lord *has* torn the heavens open and come down. Do not be frightened to face the reality, he says, particularly the reality of ourselves related to God and others. Why do people find it difficult to express their own reality or their beliefs, or even to be quiet and attentive and alone long enough to know what those things are? It should not frighten us, for, as Isaiah has just assured us, we are all the work of the Lord, Our Father.

Sleeping is just fine. We need to sleep. Escapist pursuits for recreation and rest may lead to a fuller life. But sleep or induced unconsciousness or numbness of mind as a way of life is quite another thing. Work, sleep, alcohol, drugs, gambling, constant talk or constant lack of communication so that I will not face reality, are a flight from self, from life, from God.

Those things can play their part in a full life but they are not the center of life or a distraction from living. Jesus asks us to stay attentive to the real center, to God within and the person created in God's image—to the real me. I can do this only by giving time to it—time to be with God within me.

Then, to a person thus aware, things will be seen in their context and for their relative importance. It is not by accident that distracted people are easily upset by things of no real importance and that people aware of and conscious to the great reality, while being hurt or surprised or pleased with trivia, can soon adjust by seeing it all as trivia.

Jesus wants us to be thus aware. He wants us to know deeply and totally, "Lord, you are our Father, we the clay, you the Potter, we are all the work of your hand."

Second Sunday of Advent

"The beginning of the Good News about Jesus Christ the Son of God."

Advent began by Jesus calling us to pay attention: to stay awake. Today we see the reason for that. We need to be prepared to receive the Good News.

You know, as well as I, that all people do not receive the message of Christianity as good news. Recently I heard of a politician saying that people had to be protected from Christianity.

What has gone wrong that the beautiful message of Jesus can be seen as a menace to society?

We know from the earliest records of the Church that things can go wrong. People can preach a false message, hear a false message, give an example that is contrary to the message, or simply reject the message because it interferes with their own selfish pursuits.

The true message of Jesus is indeed good news, but it will not work among selfish people because Jesus is concerned with the good of all.

We need constant preparation to receive that sort of message.

We may even have missed the message today, that in the first sentence of Mark's Gospel we are told that this is going to be "about Jesus Christ the Son of God." Have we lived so long with that idea that it has become stale to us? Jesus Christ the human being is Son of God. This is about something he has to say to us and for us. And it is Good News.

John the Baptist then tells us how we are to prepare ourselves so that this good news will always remain exciting, fresh and life-giving.

A man told me once that he went to a counselor and after a period of time came to see something in himself he had not seen before. The counselor told him that he had seen this from the start.

"Why didn't you tell me and save me all this time?"

"You would not have taken any notice. You had to come to see and accept it for yourself. Now that you own the knowledge you will do something about it."

John the Baptist tells us to prepare a way for the Lord. We need listening, open minds and hearts to hear, understand and own the message. One thing that always closes minds and hearts is sin. To be able to take the message to heart, the screens created by sin need to be removed. Sin is a looking and striving in the wrong direction and always involves selfishness: what I want to do is more important than the feelings and rights of others.

John says repent, be converted, turn around, look at things in God's way—the way of the one who loves you and loves the other. John not only said this but lived it. There is nothing in his way to prevent his mind and heart from being open to God, through Jesus. He is not concerned about making more money than other people or looking better than them or outwitting them. He is not using human beings as toys for power or profit or sexual pleasure. His mind, thus liberated, is able to see that "someone is following him, someone who is more powerful that I am, and I am not fit to kneel down and undo the straps of his sandals."

John is not the center of the universe, God is; and others, too, play their part in God's plan.

When we know this in our mind and heart, and live it, we not only have received the good news—we are the good news. Jesus the Good News lives through us.

Third Sunday of Advent

"A man sent by God. His name was John. He came as a witness."

Let us try putting our name in there. A man/woman sent by God. His/her name is. … He/she came as a witness so that everyone might believe.

But who am I? I am not the Christ, or Elijah or one of the prophets. No, like John the Baptist, I am none of these. Like John the Baptist, though, I am called to be a witness to the light. I am called to enlighten my fellow human beings to the fact that truth, honesty, unselfishness, pure love are life-giving and liberating. I am called to pour pure water of forgiveness on an unforgiving world.

It is only Jesus who can anoint with the Spirit. It is only God who can give human beings a share in his divine life. But those anointed with his life can prepare the way.

Like John the Baptist, we have limits. We can only do so much. But being incapable of doing everything does not excuse us from doing something. Our contribution may seem so insignificant against such overwhelming odds. The task of overcoming evil in the world or even some fault in ourselves, or the conversion of someone dear to us, may seem so daunting that we see no hope.

The fact that John the Baptist was a voice crying in the wilderness did not sap his hope. He spoke of and pointed to the Messiah, as God had called him to do. Light was offered to the world. He had to cry out in witness that everyone might believe through him.

If we respond to the Spirit, who has anointed us with life, we, too, will be witnesses. But we, too, must accept the feeling of being a voice in the wilderness.

When we speak and work and live the unselfish life that brings good news to the poor, binds up broken hearts, proclaims liberty to captives of greed and selfishness, we, too, will be a light shining in the darkness.

The voice in the wilderness is the unpopular voice that calls us to give up something we possess because there are those who have nothing. That voice may call people to give back land unjustly taken and never surrendered, to share their rich country with dispossessed refugees, to pay more taxes or to give generously so that the poor may have shelter, food and water. It is a voice that speaks of a human life that is more than instant satisfaction, but is everlasting.

It is a voice expressing the love that the Eternal Word has for all children of his Father. It is a voice that calls to unending love. It is a voice that reflects the love of the Divine Word who would have us live as he did, die as he did, in love with God and his brothers and sisters. It is a voice that speaks of the Word who is one with the Father and calls us to that unity now and forever.

Fourth Sunday of Advent

Last week the Church called our attention to one who co-operated with God's plan. John the Baptist prepared a way for the Lord by being what God called him to be. He wanted to be no more, no less. This he clearly stated, accepted and lived. This life of total integrity was a sign of God's powerful presence working in human nature. The presence and power of God in human beings was to be completely realized in Jesus, Emmanuel, God–with–us. It would be impossible to believe that human nature could be called to such heights had not God revealed this to us.

Today we contemplate the beginning of that wonder. "The Holy Spirit will come upon you and the Most High will cover you with its shadow. And so the child will be called holy and will be called the son of God."

Mysterious and wonderful, too, is that, here again, a mere human being is invited to co-operate. "Let what you have said be done to me." Mary became the first Christian by this "yes" to the presence of Christ in her life. "And the angel left her." As any other Christian, she then set out on the unknown journey. The yes to God is not a yes to a clear future, worked out and presented by angels. She is, as any Christian is, reliant on the Holy Spirit, the gift of God. She is to live by faith, hope and love. The details about how faith, hope and love will be best expressed will only emerge as life unfolds. We should not invent fables about Mary. She is not any of the statues or paintings we have become accustomed to. She was a flesh and blood woman in a small town in Galilee. Her earthly life was limited by time and place. The final sentence of today's reading has significance for me. "The angel left her." She is one with us.

An event unknown to the world at large in an obscure place involving a young woman changed the destiny of humankind. So-called important events of the world are sur- rounded by pomp and pageantry. Here in this sublime event, it is not the world and the flesh that give greatness, but the spirit. If ever we are able to achieve greatness as individuals, as a nation, or as a community of nations, we must first know and live by this truth. No matter what power of any kind we pos- sess, it is the spirit that determines the direction of that power. The spirit gives life.

We too, like Mary, are called to say yes to God. We are to make the Spirit present, so that again in every time and place the Word will become flesh and live among us. God's plan has not changed. He still chooses to depend on us for the power of the Most High to cover us with its shadow. We are called to be people of the Spirit, seeing beyond the immediate, partial good and saying to God, "let what you have said be done to me." We are invited to co-operate in God's plan of lasting, universal good.

As Mary did, we hope to say yes to God and travel in faith, hope and love. No angel or guiding light will lead us except the light of God's Word leading us kindly, step by step. We are a voice of that word to others and they to us.

Christmas, Mass at Dawn

We can go so fast at Christmas time and even on Christmas Day that we only scratch the surface. In fact the false surface of Christmas may even scratch us and make us very irritable. I find it very jarring to hear Christians say, "I hate Christmas." I suppose this means that they have been dragged, by custom, into doing lots of things that their hearts are not in: things such as, "He gave me a present, now I'll have to get him one" and "At least you can go to Mass on Christmas Day."

"Mary treasured all these things and pondered them in her heart." They, of course, were not the things I have just mentioned. May I invite you, even for a little while, to ponder the mystery of the great reality we celebrate today.

Ponder St Paul's words, "He did this so that we should be justified by his grace, to become heirs looking forward to inheriting eternal life." Treasure in our heart that God has come to invite us into a relationship of love with himself, the Absolute. He wants something beautiful and eternal to happen between us and himself. This can begin now, for his love is our love, his concerns ours. See how naturally it follows, then, that we love, respect and care for all his children. See, too, how this demanding love requires that we draw from the strength of his life and love. This union is his Christmas gift.

It was in the silence of the night and the stillness of the countryside that the shepherds were able to hear. Can we be still enough and listen enough to be in touch with ourselves, with the feelings of others and with God? Christmas invites us to do this.

In the silence the shepherds heard but also listened. They learned that there is more to life than the limited things we can see and touch. They left these things and found the source of all reality. Let Christmas inspire us to look deeper, to be more generous, to forgive, to seek God in prayer, to investigate our questions and doubts about him, to share some thoughts with another. Our positive responses could lead us to the great reality they found. Often we ignore the invitation to go deeper because of the business at hand, even though it may be mere trivia. Going into the darkness of the unknown, as the shepherds did, may be too risky. The shepherds went, looked, shared, learned, changed, then returned to their given tasks, but as changed people, glorifying God. Life now had a meaning.

Can the wonder of today enter a little deeper into our own being and free us too? Fear holds people back from being with, talking about, praying to and glorifying God with full hearts and firm voices.

Perhaps if we treasured the wonder in our hearts we would come to know of our own unique beauty, the unique call to each of us to become like Jesus by the way we live and love: the extraordinary call to be one with the Absolute, now and forever.

The Feast of the Holy Family

This act of religion, the offering to God of the firstborn Jesus, for Mary and Joseph was not merely ritual. It was a ceremony required by the law, as Luke tells us. Surrounded by its prescriptions and ritual, it was, perhaps, for many, a mere ritual. Parents offered their child to God and took him back into their arms, their care, their way of life, their will.

In this case the child is given into the arms of an apparent stranger. He falls into the hands of a prophet, an upright man on whom the Holy Spirit had rested. Perhaps we have presumed that Simeon was the Temple official. However, it seems that he was a devout man in Jerusalem who was called to the Temple on that day, not by an officer or duty to the law, but by the Holy Spirit. His authority came, not from the Temple, but from the Spirit of God. Here was the beginning of the creation of the new Temple, not made by human hands, that will be raised up on the last day.

Here we look in admiration at the faithful in the persons of Mary and Joseph. Called from Galilee to Bethlehem and then to Jerusalem and settling in Nazareth, they follow the will of God through exile and back. Love and union in Jesus unite them.

Mary had pondered in her heart the wonders of Christmas; now she sees, only obscurely, some dangers ahead. All who love know that true love and concern imply unselfish giving and involvement in the joys and suffering of the beloved. Being intimately involved with one who loves all is a risk that Mary and Joseph were warned of here, but accepted. They were told that their little one would be the light to the pagans and the glory of Israel, but also a sign to be rejected and a source of pain to those who loved him.

As with the shepherds, the prophets of Jesus are not those approved by the establishment, but people open to the Spirit. Simeon and Anna, people of Jerusalem, people of prayer, love of God and willingness to listen, see and hear and then proclaim the message. There is free exchange between these holy people, Mary, Joseph, Simeon and Anna. The open and free exchange of light, faith and knowledge brings a truth that may not always be easy to hear or comfortable to accept, but since it is a truth it will lead eventually to a share in the maturity, wisdom and favor of God enjoyed by Jesus.

The Epiphany of the Lord

"Lord, every nation on earth will adore you." This, the Gospel proclaims with absolute clarity. There is no one people chosen because of race, blood, birth, inheritance, brilliance of mind or any other human thing. God has no favorites. The proclamation of the good news is for everyone. The chosen ones are those who hear the word of God and keep it.

As the Christmas story has unfolded we have seen the kingdom being built up. It comes gently, quietly, through ordinary people. So far we have a young lady from a small town, a small time tradesman, a few shepherds, Simeon and Anna who are prayerful citizens of Jerusalem. As if this were not enough to try the intelligence of those who love their own power and use it to promote themselves: now we have people from outside, foreigners who have no right to be here. These men are from across the border somewhere to the east. They are not us.

They, however, like the others in the Christmas story, hear, listen, reflect, express wonder. They, like the others, undertake a journey. It is not merely a journey from place to place, but a journey of the mind, of opinion, of beliefs. It becomes a journey of the heart. Like the others, they also return eventually to where they were geographically, but not to where they were spiritually. They go by a different way. They, like the others, are changed people. They have experienced God's call to be loved and to love. Today's feast declares that no one is excluded from this call.

The inclusion of Herod's sad figure in the story is an example of those who have the opportunity to become really great, but consider their own greatness and power threatened by truth. He hears about Jesus but, it seems, never comes to know him. Their stories never come together because of fear.

The message of the Epiphany is that God wants to show forth his love to all, without exception. But love must be returned if it is to achieve its end—the happiness of the beloved. In Herod fear would not let love in. His position, prestige and comfort seem to have killed the spirit that would have enabled him to see beyond the shortness of his life and the limits of his human existence. For such a one, everything, eventually, must become mundane and dull.

For the Wise Men and those around the crib life became an adventure. "The sight of the star filled them with delight." Life became a delightful journey into the Unknown, whom they would see and know in Jesus.

On this feast of God's universal love the child Jesus beckons us into a deeper union with God through him. May the sight of the star of hope lead us into a life of meaning—a life of loving union with God, the Universal Lover.

The Baptism of the Lord

In today's liturgy we pick up and continue the theme of the Epiphany. God reveals his chosen one. "Pay attention, come to me, listen and your soul will live." God calls us to look and listen. Last week the shining star and the enlightenment of men from the East: this week, John the Baptist, the human instrument of God, points the way. Last week the men from the east fell on their knees before the child who is God, today the holy man of the desert directs us to the One he is not even worthy to kneel before. The events were separated by thirty years as far as time is concerned, but God calls each in the way he wants and at the time he chooses.

God is present in all times and places in the Spirit, the water and the blood. This flesh and blood human being, one with the elements, one with us, is the Beloved of God, Son of God, carrying our human nature into the favor of God.

The Epiphany, the showing forth of God among us, took place in Bethlehem and at the Jordan and in every word, gesture and action of Jesus. But, by the Spirit, the water and the blood, God brings each of us into the life of Jesus. Every act of love, generosity and forgiveness shows forth the presence of God until the end of time. By the redeeming blood of Christ each of us, through the water of the Baptism, receives the Spirit. We live with the same Spirit as Jesus. As Jesus walked freely into the water he symbolically plunged into our humanity. There was nothing human he would avoid. He was, and still is, with our human condition in all things except sin. He calls us to embrace fully this unity with him.

God's overwhelming love spoke out, confirming, embracing, acknowledging the wonder of this unity of divine and human nature. The Eternal love of the Father for his Son spoke out in time for this Son now immersed in time, and in part of human history. The Son, loved in Eternity, one with the Father, is loved in time as one with humanity. "You are my son, the beloved; my favor rests on you."

Now, as we Christians, Christ-bearers, carry Christ into our own time and place, as we live by the Spirit and identify with his love, the voice of the Father embraces us and resonates in our hearts, "You are my beloved child, the beloved; my favor rests on you."

First Sunday
of Lent

By signs and words Ash Wednesday reminded us of the origin and the destiny of our visible existence. Our bodies are of the elements common to all visible things and will disintegrate.

In today's Gospel we are called to, "Repent and believe in the Good News." Life as we know it will end but there is good news. God calls us to an indescribably fuller and happier life. God offers us union with himself "through the resurrection of Jesus Christ who has entered heaven."

The first Sunday of Lent reminds us of the earthly struggle with evil, but also of the victory over evil.

This is the point of the Noah story. The book of Genesis, from which the story comes, is about God, the loving Creator, and about our response to his love. The selfishness which is sin leads to alienation from God, from our inner selves and from each other. It leads to destruction. We do not need much reflection to realize that the story is still with us.

However, the Noah story and other Genesis stories also emphasize God's enduring patience and love. In the fourth Eucharistic Prayer we say to God "again and again you offered a covenant." Here in the Noah story is another instance of God's covenant. God's promise to save is never withdrawn.

A consolation today for those who struggle against the odds to be faithful, is the message of the Noah story that a few can make the difference.

Jesus traveled the journey of the few. He experienced the destructive force of evil in the loneliness of temptation. Those who have felt a little of what he felt during that forty days will know the meaning of "in the wilderness." It was through the desert of facing this human experience and of overcoming it that the consolation of God's power and love was felt. Jesus then was at peace with God, with himself and with nature, "he was with the wild beasts and the angels looked after him."

Coming through that desolation and experiencing the power of God over evil, he was able to proclaim with conviction and feeling, "The time has come and the kingdom of God is close at hand. Repent and believe in the Good News."

The covenants between God and his people, expressing his love and saving power have reached their pinnacle. Here is the final covenant. God's final sign is no other than Emmanuel—God–with–us. In Jesus the sign of God's presence is God's presence in human flesh.

At the beginning of Lent we already look towards Easter and the water of Baptism by which we were filled with God's presence. Through the observance of Lent we hope to renew the wonder of that gift.

Second Sunday of Lent

Surely the reason so many people reject, or are sceptical about, Christianity is that they have been exposed to a mere caricature of Christ's teaching.

"He warned them to tell no one what they had seen, until the son of man has risen from the dead." These words from today's gospel should be taken seriously today. The true message is the whole message.

The disciples had just come into contact with a world beyond normal experience. By a mystical experience they had glimpsed for a while the wonder of Jesus. This man who walked, talked and ate with them was greater than Moses and Elijah. The law of Moses and the prophetic teaching of Elijah are at his service. These were to be perfected and given life in Jesus. Here, standing with them, was the image of the Father, "My Son, the Beloved," and the one the world needed to hear: "Listen to Him."

No wonder the disciples had to be warned to restrain their enthusiasm. This was not the final glory to be preached. The story had not yet unfolded completely. They were to "listen to him" and observe him, to go through Good Friday and all that led up to it. Then they could observe and preach the glorified one. It was when they had full experience of what "Son of Man" meant that "risen from the dead" would have its full meaning. Half the message would be a distorted message.

It was only step by step that Abraham finally saw what God had in store for him and Isaac. Abraham believed that only good could come from doing God's will. This belief enabled him to go forward, step by step. It was this faith that brought the abundant blessings.

It is this patient faith that Jesus requires of his disciples: "Tell no one until...." God has his time and way to complete the revelation of what today foreshadows.

The Christian message can not be understood in a piecemeal way. To look upon Christianity as a set of rules or obligations or as a set of duties to be performed is a caricature of its beauty. People often talk of religion as "pie in the sky." This, too, is a caricature. Jesus did not leave us such legacies.

Jesus brought his friends down from the mountain renewed in faith and with fresh vigor to face the realities of life on earth. It is by his being truly "Son of Man," immersed in the troubles and complexities of life, undergoing its sufferings and facing the inevitable, that he enables us to be sons and daughters of God.

Eventually it was those who were truly risen with Jesus who were sent to teach and witness. Having listened, suffered, known the need for forgiveness, they had, with Jesus, died and risen. They knew and lived the risen Christ.

False messages come from half truth and wrong emphasis. False messages also come from those who preach and profess the truth but contradict it with their lives.

It is when "the Son of Man is risen from the dead" in the words and actions and whole life of his disciples that the full truth will be recognized and loved.

Third Sunday of Lent

When we celebrated the Feast of the Holy Family earlier this year, we read from Luke's Gospel that Mary and Joseph took Jesus to the Temple to consecrate him to the Lord and offer a pair of turtle doves or two young pigeons. Although that event took place some thirty years before today's Gospel episode, it is reasonable to assume that Mary and Joseph had dealings with the pigeon sellers. There was only one Temple. In today's Gospel those pigeon sellers are told by Jesus, "Take all this out of here and stop turning my Father's house into a market."

Mary and Joseph were obeying the law, acting as they were expected to act as good Jews. It is impossible to believe that they saw anything but virtue in their activity that day. I suppose it was the same with the people buying and selling there on this day and the people selling the beasts to be offered in sacrifice. They may have asked Jesus, "what has it got to do with you? We are doing no harm." Those words sound familiar, but people who ask them usually don't want an answer.

Jesus, on the contrary, saw the incongruity of it. He saw that something originally meant to bring people closer to God had been profaned. The original purpose of the law had been obscured by outward show. Worse still, people were intent on making money and gaining financial advantage from privileged positions.

Let us leave the scene and come to today's temple. In today's Gospel Jesus calls our attention to real temples. The meeting place between God and humanity is the real presence of God and humanity in Jesus. The holiest place on earth is no longer a stone building but a human person.

As Jesus is the Temple of God, so also are his followers. Every person is a sacred creation of God. His presence, his Spirit, dwells in his followers. Jesus has assured us that we are one with him, that we are home to the Father, that his Spirit is our gift. After his resurrection his apostles passed on the same message—we are the Temple of God. No longer is the Temple confined to any particular time or place, it is wherever God is worshiped in Spirit and in truth.

Let us invite Jesus to walk into these temples of my inner self and your inner self. Is Jesus at home with the activity there? Is this the Father's house of prayer? Does he have to drive out things he cannot live with? Am I comfortable to have Jesus as my guest, walking freely, as I am engaged in this act of worship right now?

Perhaps the most disturbing part of this exercise is to reflect about what I have said about the people buying and selling in the Temple that day in Jerusalem. They did not see anything wrong with the things that made Jesus angry. Worse still, they don't seem to have asked him what was wrong with their activity. They asked him for a sign to justify his actions. So they forgot the critic and got on with the job.

We need to be better listeners than this. Perhaps a test of whether my temple needs cleansing is to ask myself whether I think Jesus would be at home worshiping in my temple. He is surrounded, not by money changers, but by my attitudes. I mean attitudes of revenge or of forgiveness, of unjust and unintelligent discrimination, or of seeking to understand and accept difference; attitudes of bitterness, or of aspirations of hope and prayer for the well-being of all.

Perhaps we will discover the wonder of what our temple is if we have the courage to share what we find with someone else. Where two or three are gathered in his name, Jesus is present.

Fourth Sunday of Lent

John begins the story of the meeting between Jesus and Nicodemus with the words, "There was one of the Pharisees, called Nicodemus, a leading Jew, who came to Jesus by night and said, 'Rabbi, we know that you are a teacher who comes from God.'"

Just before that, John told of the cleansing of the Temple by Jesus (last Sunday's Gospel). It is significant that John placed these stories together.

Jesus, who feared no one, walked into the Temple in broad daylight in full view of anyone who cared to observe his actions and hear his words. For him, one thing was important. It was not his popularity or any desire to be accepted and respected by the "in-people." It was that God deserves the best we can give. His honor would be compromised if we made sure we wouldn't lose anything by serving him.

Nicodemus, by contrast, came to Jesus at night time. In coming out of the darkness of uncertainty he had already, by faith, taken a step into the unknown he was seeking. He acknowledged Jesus and began the search of his life. Yet he kept his options open. Under the cover of darkness he was still able to go back to the security of being "a leading Jew." It seems he was not yet prepared to risk everything.

Then the depths of God's generosity and love were brought to light. Jesus revealed to this man the wonder of the extent to which God will go to bring us eternal life.

No, Nicodemus is not condemned. No one is condemned when a step is taken into the light, even a cautious, tentative step. "For God sent his son into the world, not to condemn the world, but so that through him the world might be saved."

Then came the appeal to Nicodemus, and to us all, to come into the light fully and freely; to live lives that need no cover of darkness; to live lives that speak the truth in all their deeds and words and reverent silence. "The man who lives by the truth comes out into the light, so that it may be plainly seen that what he does is done in God."

Such integrity could cost Nicodemus all that was dear to him Such integrity cost Jesus social acceptance, friends, immense mental and physical pain, and life itself. By the strength of the Spirit he promised, his followers would come into the light, live by the truth and show up the power of darkness for what it is. Like Jesus, they will suffer the consequences. For the power of darkness uses the destructive weapons of evil which followers of Jesus must reject. Their power is the power of truth, integrity, peace and love. It is a power that comes not from taking up arms of destruction but by laying down life for the life of the world.

Jesus is still "a light that shines in the darkness" but "a light that darkness could not overpower." (John 1:5)

Fifth Sunday of Lent

It is disconcerting when we say something and get back a reply that has nothing to do with what we said. We, too, have probably made inappropriate responses because, being distracted, we have not given sufficient attention to another.

The reply that Jesus gave to Andrew and Philip sounds a bit like this. They told him of some prospective disciples and he seemed to talk about something else that was on his mind.

Perhaps there is a deeper meaning here, an invitation to see him in a way they had never imagined.

We too would like to see Jesus. But seeing Jesus is not something to do with the time and place we occupy in history or with visions. Seeing Jesus in a way that will make a difference to life has to do with the reply he gave to Andrew and Philip here.

When we wish to see Jesus, whom are we looking for? Is it someone to satisfy our curiosity, to answer our prayers, to supply our presumed needs, to prove we are right in our beliefs, to show others that they should have known better?

If we and those Greeks want to see Jesus, Son of God, Son of Mary, we will have to look life in the face—watch it drop into the ground and die—all the while believing that God will glorify the same life, lifting it up.

The letter to the Hebrews tells us that God answered Christ's prayer in this way. "Christ offered up prayer and entreaty aloud and in silent tears to the one who had power to save him out of death … his prayer was heard." But it was heard in the same way that the request of the Greeks was heard. They would see Jesus as he was through the reality of life, suffering and death. God heard the prayer of Jesus in a totally unexpected way. God did not preserve his human life and save it from suffering and death, but saved the whole of humanity and raised it up through and from these very things.

The richness of life comes from living the life we are given. "Anyone who loves his life loses it. Anyone who hates his life in this world will keep it for eternal life." Seeing beyond the immediate, knowing life for what it is—flesh and spirit, communion with all creation and the Creator—will cause the followers of Christ to be lost to self-centered living and to merely saving what they possess. The fear of losing something will not stop them from living to the full. Christians, those who have seen Jesus, will live as he did, growing in life as life is broken and shared with others and with God in trust and prayer. Their entreaty, too, will be in words and deeds and in tears shed silently for the injustices that continue, despite their efforts for the afflicted.

These Greeks, representing the outsiders and those on the fringe, will be part of the answer to the great prayer of the Cross, "And when I am lifted up from the earth, I shall draw all to myself." They are not forgotten outsiders. There are no forgotten outsiders.

Passion Sunday

Love expressed by gift-giving is as old and as universal as memory. Consider, then, the love God has for us. His gift is his Eternal Son, God himself.

In this special week we try to contemplate, as best we can, what that gift implies. What special love is here, for no gift can be compared to the gift of God himself. God came to our house to invite us to his home. He became one of us to invite us to be one with him. He lived the human life so that we may share the eternal divine life of God.

There is the gift. The price of the gift is that God became human and took all that being human implies. He held nothing back. Being human, Jesus had to be born, to eat, feel, go through growing up, develop relationships, experience love and understanding, but also hatred and misunderstanding, faithlessness and betrayal, suffering and death. His birth as a human being implied his death, as it does for all of us. All earthly things that live must die. Jesus was, by gift of God to us, an earthly thing. He was totally committed to the human condition.

By accepting the will of the Father, Jesus accepted human life. His total fidelity to the Father prevented him from refusing death. It is not strange, then, that Jesus spoke of the will of the Father in relation to his death. God did not want people to kill Jesus. He did want to invite us to himself through Jesus, showing the love for what he had created. He wanted Jesus to bring us to him. He did this in an extraordinarily loving way. "God so loved the world that he gave his only Son." The gift is total, never revoked. Since his Son was born a human being, God accepted his death.

The wonderful integrity of Jesus in the face of the evil and selfish attitudes of people led to the events we read about today. Sin causes suffering. Those who stand up against injustice, dishonesty or evil in any of its forms will suffer. God does not want suffering, but asks us to suffer rather than to allow the suffering caused by evil to continue and multiply. This is why Jesus had to suffer in this way. In his stand he was doing the will of the Father.

It was not the pain, the blood, the hurtful loneliness, the distress brought to his Mother and friends that pleased God in the death of Jesus. It was his faithfulness. Again it is the spirit that makes the difference. The world is redeemed by the faithfulness of Jesus, consisting of a total life and everything said and done, through to torture and death.

In all of this God is loved, trusted, put first and totally honored by the spirit of Jesus. The human spirit has reached its heights and triumphed in Jesus. In this God triumphs over evil.

The Easter Vigil

Here and now we celebrate the wonder of God's presence in the past, present and future.

The word of God you have just read, takes us back through history and still further back. For we have recalled those things we can know only by reason or revelation. From reason we know that, because we depend for our existence on something outside ourselves, ultimately we have to have an origin which did not come into existence by itself. From revelation we have come to know and love a caring God who is the ultimate origin.

The book of Genesis is not telling us how or when created things came to be. It is stating that we came to be from one who is all good. Seven times in this story of creation we are told that God's creation is good. The message of the goodness of all things is driven home to people who contend with forces both good and evil. God is the force of loving creation. His creation is from love for love. He is good. It is good.

We are the image of this creative goodness. We, then, are to live as people of creative love. It is this creative, loving response to God and his creation that will bring his plan to fruition. His gifts are spread through his creation to be shared.

It is through the selfish choice to go our own way that God's plan is frustrated. The Scriptures give us examples of sin and its consequences.

However, God does not abandon us. He keeps assuring us of his care. He keeps calling us back to his way out of slavery and alienation that result from selfishness.

The Exodus story is one such reminder. Fear, jealousy and pride enslaved a people. God does not want those he created free to be enslaved. He is the liberator. He stands by the oppressed even when things seem hopeless.

All these Scripture accounts of God's faithful love lead up to his great act of liberation. He, himself, comes to us. He confronts sin even when it is evil enough to attempt to destroy goodness itself.

In Jesus God plunges into his own creation and becomes a creature. He accepts the situation as it is. He enters the sinful human world and suffers the consequences. The consequences of sin are always worse for those who attempt to overcome the evil. Thus the consequences for Jesus were drastic. Goodness is called evil and evil is called an act of God. Jesus is tortured and killed.

God will not let evil overcome good. It may seem to triumph. This is illusion and short-lived. The Resurrection of Jesus is the great sign that God cares, loves and sees us through. It is more. In the death of Jesus the impossible has been attempted. Human beings cannot destroy God. Still more: in the resurrection of Jesus, a human being is united with God in eternal life. The wonder and joy for us is that in and through Jesus we humans have a new destiny. Human nature is carried into the divine life. We belong with God in eternal, beatific life. "If in union with God we have imitated his death, we shall also imitate his resurrection."

We have the joy of celebrating this union which exists here and now. By our worship, our love, our renewal of baptism and our commitment to bringing light to the world, we deepen what we celebrate.

We celebrate too, the future. All we recall tonight in these holy acts and all that we receive is directed towards the wonder of its outcome. The wonder is life as Jesus lived it and the life of eternal joy.

Second Sunday of Easter

Even wise people share with the animal kingdom the instinct to fight or to fly in face of danger. They may even react without thought when threatened. But truly wise people are not bound and ruled to abide by their instinctive reactions. They will not feel committed to standing by an instinctive act that was inappropriate.

If someone catches us off guard with a hurtful act, either physically or psychologically, we are prone to sudden reaction. The foolish person will feel committed to that action and will seek ways of confirming it to justify the conduct. Wise people, after reflection, will come to the decision that violence and revenge are not appropriate. Rather than confirming any bitterness, they will seek reconciliation. If animal instinct took over for an instant, they will seek a response more appropriate to a human being.

On a higher level still, Jesus gives human beings the capacity and power to forgive. Forgiveness is a Christian gift which we are capable of exercizing with the power of Christ.

In today's Gospel scene, not only does Jesus give us the power to forgive, but the whole passage is one of forgiveness and reconciliation. It tells of first reactions and then of later thoughtful responses.

In face of danger the disciples fled from the scene of the capture and crucifixion of Jesus. Then Thomas's reaction to being left out and getting second-hand knowledge of the risen

Christ is recorded. He was probably hurt and disappointed. He certainly expressed disbelief.

But in both cases there was a reflection and another response. The disciples, having fled, now gathered, even though they were still frightened. Thomas, after his forthright statement, was back with the other disciples a week later.

This is in contrast to another group of people and another individual disciple. The chief priests and rulers, having seen to the death of Jesus, even though given time, bribed the guards to say someone had stolen the body of Jesus. They thought over and confirmed their wrongdoing. Judas did not give either himself or Jesus a second chance to make things right.

We are presented with Jesus standing with his walking wounded. He is not the bearer of revenge or the messenger who tells them that this is their last chance. He says nothing of that. He brings peace. If they are at peace with God they are totally forgiven, reconciled, restored. In fact he even goes further. He trusts them with more and gives them greater dignity than ever.

As Jesus spoke for God and pronounced God's forgiveness, they were honored with the same mission. They were disciples, now they are apostles. As he was sent, now they are sent.

This risen Christ we receive in Holy Communion. To us he holds out welcoming arms, hands wounded for us. To us he says, "Peace, there is nothing to fear." He fills us with his power to forgive, to be in his presence, as he says to us, "Receive the Holy Spirit."

Third Sunday of Easter

The acknowledgment of sins, faults, needs and weaknesses is necessary for one who is to be a herald of the Gospel. We begin each mass with such an acknowledgment to God and to the community. We confess our need for forgiveness and we accept forgiveness.

St Peter spoke with authority in proclaiming the resurrection of Jesus. There was no compromise in his preaching the truth about Jesus. He did not cover up the facts in order to win favor with the people, "who demanded the reprieve of a murderer while you killed the prince of life." There was no compromise in proclaiming, "God raised him from the dead and to that fact we are witnesses." For the bearer of God's message there can be no compromise with the truth.

The other side of the true prophet is also revealed in Peter's address. Wrong is always wrong, but God is the only one capable of the judgment that the wrong action is sinful. It was here that Peter, while firm with the truth, is gentle and compassionate. Their action was wrong. "You demanded the reprieve of a murderer while you killed the prince of life." But compassion is shown to those involved in the wrongdoing. Peter gave his hearers room to move. He refused to pile guilt upon guilt as he excused them—"Neither you nor your leaders had any idea what you were really doing." They were not innocent, but their position was far from impossible. He assured them, "Now you must repent and turn to God, so that your sins may be wiped out." God was waiting for them, not to condemn but to forgive and embrace with love and life.

Here spoke Peter the apostle of truth. Here spoke Peter, repentant sinner himself. He spoke from his experience of the resurrection. Peter also spoke from his experience of sin, ignorance and glorious and complete forgiveness. He has been where they are. He invited them to where he was.

We see from the Gospel the difficulty the disciples had experienced in accepting the fact of the resurrection themselves. It is from this very weakness that the fact of the resurrection is more definitely established and confirmed. From openly expressing their doubts and disbelief, the disciples came to share the experience of others who doubted. At the same time they gradually learned of the many times that Jesus had appeared and the many ways that he had shown his presence. In sharing weakness and doubt they gained strength and knowledge from each other.

As if frustrated as to know how often and how definite he had to be in his presence, Jesus kept making it clearer. Here they saw, heard, touched and even ate with him. He guided them through the Scriptures and let them see to what the Scriptures pointed. In seeing the risen Christ they saw the point and meaning of all that had gone before. The resurrection is our human destiny.

Now they were ready. Having sinned, they had experienced forgiveness; having doubted, they had been confirmed in faith and knowledge. In every sense they had experienced the risen Lord. They had assurance from their Lord that they could give what they had received. "You are witnesses to this."

Fourth Sunday of Easter

When Jesus described himself as the Good Shepherd he told us that we are worth dying for. His love for us involves total commitment of life till the end. "I am the Good Shepherd," then he gives the consequence, "The Good Shepherd is one who lays down his life for his sheep." His love of the Father involves the Father's love for his children. The commitment to the will of the Father means commitment to those whom the Father loves. We are involved in the eternal love of the Holy Trinity. The will of God is the happiness of his children. "This is the command I have been given by my Father."

We are the reason for the human existence of Jesus. John, whose words we have just read, began his Gospel by telling us that the Word who became flesh, this Good Shepherd, exists eternally with the Father. Through him all things have their being. The Son, God himself, has no need in himself to become human. He takes up human life and lays it down so that we may live to the full. In the resurrection he takes it up so that we are taken up, in, with and through him.

The laying down of his life is not solely in the crucifixion but in the gift of his whole life for us. His birth, teaching, suffering, death, resurrection and ascension are for us. "I know my own and my own know me, just as the Father knows me and I know the Father." By living among us and teaching us, Jesus brings us into the life of the Holy Trinity, giving new life to the nature God has made in his own image. The knowledge of the Father, Son and Holy Spirit, which is eternal love, is communicated to us. We are free to embrace it. Through the wonder of a response of faith, hope and love, we partake in this knowledge-love of God. The divine being dwells in us.

Here is no shepherd tending the flock for his own ends. This is not a shepherd who wields the rod of authoritative force to bring his flock into subservient conformity. The sheep do not exist for the shepherd. The shepherd takes on human existence for the sheep. He calls them into life and freedom.

Jesus came to redeem us and bring us to God. But since we are one body with the Good Shepherd we, too, participate in his redeeming activity. We are shepherds with him.

Being one with Christ, the Good Shepherd, we look with sorrow, but also with hope and love, on sheep without a shepherd and on those "other sheep I have that are not of this fold." We realize that if they are to hear his voice, it is through us that they will hear it. It is a voice expressing the love of the Father, sometimes heard in teaching, sometimes in words of real concern for justice and love, sometimes in words of consolation and generous forgiveness. It is a word written into every act of unselfish kindness. It is the silent expression of love and justice in our actions particularly for those who have little power of their own.

Followers of the Good Shepherd do not take up arms to win by force but lay down their lives in the service of love and justice.

All followers of Christ are initiated into the mission of the Good Shepherd. Some are called to devote their lives exclusively to the spreading of his word and the realization of his presence in the Holy Eucharist and in service to the least of his children. Men and women who are called are invited to lay down their lives that life may flourish and come to its destined union with God. Whoever we are, whatever our state of life or our calling, we are all one body in and with the Good Shepherd, who lays down his life for all.

Fifth Sunday of Easter

One conclusion from our reflection last week on Christ, the Good Shepherd, is that we are one with the redeeming Shepherd.

Today we listen to Jesus saying just that. Human life is to reach its God-given potential as life in union with God by our being one life with Christ. Just as a vine and its branches live with a common life principle, so the Spirit living in Jesus is the same Spirit that lifts our life into union with God.

Cast off from the divine life, we will live our little, self-centered lives producing no fruit. Like a branch without its source of life we will wither.

Life involves growth and change. It is never static. The fruit of Christ's life is a full life for those who are one with him. That same life in his followers must bear the same fruit. The branch cut off from its source of life cannot do this. The branch living with the same life as the vine fulfills the vine's destiny. A life in Christ must produce the fruit of Christ's life. "Whoever remains in me, with me in him, bears fruit in plenty; cut off from me you can do nothing."

By word and sacrament and works of love, the Spirit of Jesus lives in us. Through and in us Jesus continues to call others to this life in God. In every Christian response, every act of love, every deed of justice, in every attempt to worship the Father in spirit and in truth, the vine is bearing fruit through its branches. Through the life of Christ, expressed in

Christian living, the prayer of Christ continues to be said and fulfilled: "Thy kingdom come, Thy will be done." That kingdom is here and now and is eternal.

In the Acts of the Apostles we see the beginning of this. Jesus left the world to the care of his followers. Paul is confronted on the road to Damascus with the words, "Why are you persecuting me?" No wonder Paul's writings are so expressive of the knowledge of Christ as being one with his followers. It was his introduction to the redeeming Christ. Christ and his followers are living with the same life. Through them he is heard and loved, or persecuted and ignored.

The presence of Christ in his followers unfolds as Paul's life proceeds from this point. Ananias welcomes him with the words, "Brother Saul, I have been sent by the Lord Jesus who appeared to you on your way here so that you may recover your sight and be filled with the Holy Spirit." The Lord speaks and acts through Ananias, and Paul becomes one with Christ and with his followers. (Acts 9:17)

In today's passage from the Acts of the Apostles we see the Spirit of Jesus the reconciler and encourager working through Barnabas. His name means Son of Encouragement. This wonderful encourager trusts Paul, takes him to the apostles, introduces him, dispels fear, creates trust and brings about reconciliation. Here is the Spirit of Jesus living, speaking and healing. Barnabas, Paul, the apostles listen to the voice of Jesus speaking through his disciples and respond with love and service.

That Spirit of Jesus expresses himself in ways unknown to us as we listen to his word and respond with love and life. Since he lives in us we must bear the fruit.

Sixth Sunday of Easter

When Jesus spoke of the vine and the branches he spoke of his disciples sharing in the dynamic force that is God's life. (Last Sunday.) Sharing in this life, through union with Christ, we are made one in the Holy Spirit of God.

United with Christ in the most wonderful and complete way, Peter's ministry resembles that of Jesus. His words move people to repentance, the reception of the Spirit and union with Christ in baptism. Like Jesus, he is able to see beyond human barriers of race and nations, and to proclaim, "The truth I have come to realize is that God does not have favorites, but that anyone from any nationality who fears God and does what is right is acceptable to him."

The key to all of this is the union that exists between Christ and Peter through the gift of the Holy Spirit. The key is love. Peter's spirit is lifted into the life of God who is love.

The promise of Peter's place in the kingdom was made after a profession of faith: "You are the Christ, the Son of the living God." (Matthew 16:17) The fulfillment of the promise and the commissioning of Peter took place after a procla- mation of love, "Lord, you know everything. You know I love you." (John 21:17)

It is love which is the real test of unity with God. The more we achieve unity with God, the more we are filled with his life, which is love. In today's second reading John gives us some absolutes. Since God is love it is impossible to have his life within us without loving. It is "not our love for God but God's love for us when he sent his Son ..." This gift of God is the beginning of a new way of loving. One who is filled with the gift of God's life has the gift of that life to dispense to others. This new life is like God's own life. It is creative, life-giving, liberating. When life is in us to the full our love can never be possessive, demanding or self-centered to the point where others are lessened.

God's gift of love to us is beyond mere human capacity. Human beings love in all sorts of ways. We give all sorts of feelings and attitudes the name of love. Human nature responds in love to those who are close by blood or sympathy, or to expressions of generosity and kindness. It is attracted by physical beauty and warmth of personality. God's love is towards all. Gifted by this love we are called to love as God does, without discrimination. Rejection and misunderstanding do not diminish the love of God. It needs a divine gift to live by: "Love your enemies, do good to those who hate you; bless those who curse you and pray for those who maltreat you." (Luke 6:27) It is also a life-long task, for it goes beyond the warm human feelings towards those perceived by us to be lovable. It invites us into God's life which is pure gift to us. It is the call to live the life of grace we possess through baptism, confirmation and Eucharist.

When we live in this way, we really are God's children for, "anyone who loves is begotten by God and knows God." We know God in the sense that Jesus speaks of. It is a deep, intimate knowledge. It is the knowledge that can end only in love. Like the love that is its origin, it embraces all.

This does not mean that we have to approve all the actions of our fellow human beings. Some of these actions we must condemn as Jesus did. Love may require that we confront evil with courage, but this, too, will be done out of care for others and with care for all. Secondly, when we speak of universal love we do this in the context of our limited lives. We cannot, like God, know all. Our call is to respond with love and understanding to those whose lives cross our path in some way. Thirdly, we should never despair that we have not reached the perfect state. Life is growth and journey. Jesus calls us to want to grow and to want to take the journey that will end in life to the full. He has promised that we will be given anything we ask for in his name. Asking for this gift of loving is certainly asking in his spirit—in his name.

Seventh Sunday of Easter

"The Lord has set his sway in Heaven and his Kingdom is ruling over all." All that exists is God's creation, sustained by his loving rule. His presence is all-pervading. In the coming of Jesus, God entered our created world in an entirely different way. To created matter and human history, God's nature was married. In Jesus, God touches us in an extraordinary way. We are invited to enter this wonderful union. "The Bride of Christ" is certainly an appropriate name for the people of God, his Church. Through Christ we enter into a new relationship with God. This union implies a unity with all those united with Christ. Thus Jesus prays, "Holy Father, keep those you have given me true to your name, so that they may be one like us."

The life-giving presence of Jesus in his people continues to reach out to all, inviting them into union with God. This presence speaks to the world through those who are united with him and each other to form his body. "As you sent me into the world I have sent them into the world." Because they are his presence, Jesus prays for them. He was totally dedicated and consecrated to the truth. The continuing mission of Jesus implies dedicated followers, consecrated in truth.

In the reading of the Acts of the Apostles we see the disciples responding to the prayers of Jesus. His prayer was being fulfilled as they met in unity and love, and in concern for the kingdom. They were in touch with each other and with the

Holy Spirit as they discerned and prayed that God would fill the gap felt from the loss of Judas.

As Justus and Matthias were named and Matthias chosen to be "listed as one of the twelve," the disciples acted in the place of Jesus. The things that God did through the Word made flesh in Jesus, he continued to do through the mystical body of Jesus. Here he is looking at his disciples and selecting one from their number as he did while he was with them in the flesh. Christ continues to call and to send those called on the mission of reconciling people to God.

Justus and Matthias are not mentioned in the Gospel by name. They were, however, with Jesus "the whole time that Jesus was traveling around with us," as were the others from whom they were chosen. Those unnamed disciples were with him from the time John the Baptist named Jesus as the Lamb of God. They had remained faithful in spite of the ridicule of their religious leaders, through the terror of the crucifixion, until they experienced the joy of his resurrection and ascension. Now when one is called from their number to be "counted among the apostles" our attention is drawn to the fidelity of these unnamed disciples.

Throughout the history of the Church there has been that constant number of unnamed disciples, bearing witness and bringing Jesus present to the world. Reflect for a moment on the fidelity that brings you each Sunday to worship God through Jesus, to be enlivened by the Holy Spirit and to pray for the needs of all.

We praise God for his gift of faithful people who make up Christian communities throughout the world and through the ages. We praise him especially for our own community.

The Ascension of the Lord

In his Gospel Luke began by addressing Theophilus, that is, the one who loves God, with the assurance of the authenticity of his story about Jesus.

Today's first reading is the beginning of Luke's second contribution to the New Testament. Again he addresses Theophilus, reminding him about the first book about Jesus and introducing him to the continuing life and work of Jesus.

The life of Jesus continues as he goes to where his divine nature takes him. He goes "into heaven." It is the same Jesus that his followers have known, as recorded in the Gospel. It is this flesh and blood human being who, being one with God, now takes human nature to heaven.

Then Luke begins to tell of the continuing life of Jesus who is still with us. Although he is taken up to heaven, he lives on earth still. He continues to teach, forgive, heal, gather disciples into a community of love and service and thus to bring them into union with God. He remains to pass on the spirit that brings us into the full life that we in turn pass on to others.

St Paul, co-worker with Luke, expresses the very same thing as he speaks of the Spirit that makes the body of Christ present. The gifts that Jesus has for the world are still distributed by Jesus. They are contained in the body of Christ active on earth.

Authentic followers of Christ never see the gifts of others as a source of envy, but see them for what they are: the heart, head, hands and mind of Jesus. The authentic followers of Jesus see their own gifts as the power of the saving Jesus working through them. Gifts distributed by God so generously are not for personal power, but for service. They are power for goodness, freedom and salvation.

It is with this power that Jesus endows his disciples as he sends them to be his saving presence. "Go out to the whole world; proclaim the Good News to all creation." Whatever power they have is at the service of the Good News, in the service of others.

The disciple is not only to teach the truths about God, but to communicate God. It is not merely a matter of communicating facts but of communicating love as Jesus did. He spoke of the Loving Father, the redeeming Son, the life-giving Spirit with intense love for his subject and for those who listened. This teaching Jesus remains with us today, loving us into the life of God.

This Jesus can only be seen fully and heard fully in his Church, when and where that gathering of people is united in love of God, each other and the people to whom they are sent.

Expressing the mind of Jesus, Paul puts it thus to the Ephesians and to us. "In this way we are all to come to unity in our faith and in our knowledge of the son of God, until we become the perfect Man, fully mature with the fullness of Christ himself."

Pentecost Sunday

The outward signs of winds and fire and of hearing the word through the barriers of language differences were observed through the senses of those who experienced the first Pentecost. Yet these things that could be seen and felt and heard were the shadow of the reality that could not be seen. The unseen gift to the apostles was the real wonder. The Spirit of God, promised by Jesus, revealed the wonder that was their union with God. What they possessed already by union with Jesus, the very life of God, was confirmed in them and made known to them with such clarity that their joy, and the desire to communicate that joy, could not be contained. All fear was vanquished. The threat of being rejected, captured, imprisoned or even killed was cast out by the love that now filled their being. They had to share with all that spirit of wonder and awe at the presence of God within them. No barrier could hold them back from the proclamation and promulgation of the "marvels of God."

We think of the change that took place with the apostles at Pentecost. Perhaps it was more that they realized who they were already, what they possessed by grace and nature, what they knew from Jesus. The gifts of God they already had were now directed totally towards the kingdom that they had learned about, but which they now knew and loved. "The Spirit of truth ... will be witness and you too will be witnesses because you have been with me from the outset."

St Peter is an example of this. Before Pentecost he was already the one who stepped forward and spoke up with vehemence. But it could have been to acknowledge Christ as the Son of the Living God, to declare that he was willing to die rather that to deny Jesus, to cut off the man's ear or to deny with equal vehemence that he did not know Jesus. After Pentecost Peter is still the outspoken, enthusiastic, forthright leader. But his natural gifts are filled with God's Spirit and directed totally towards the kingdom.

It is much the same with St Paul. The vehement persecutor of the Church, when filled with God's Spirit, became equally vehement as a preacher of the Gospel.

The difference, the change, is that the various gifts of nature are directed towards the glory of God and the salvation of his people. Gifts of intellect, knowledge, personality, gifts of mind and body, are to a large extent at the disposal of the human will. They can be self-centered and destructive. They can be united with the creative Spirit of God as part of his creative plan.

Pentecost celebrates the reality that God's creative Spirit is gift to our human condition. Filled with the Holy Spirit we are ready for life with God in Heaven. Filled with the Holy Spirit, all our natural gifts are directed towards creative life. It is self-centered life that destroys. As Paul told us, "When self-indulgence is at work the results are these." He then gives examples of destructive conduct such as "sexual irresponsibility ... feuding ... jealousy ... bad temper and quarrels ... drunkenness."

The person capable of such things is also capable of openness to the Holy Spirit. "What the Spirit brings is very different: love, joy, peace, patience, kindness, goodness, trustfulness, gentleness and self control."

Pentecost invites us to say to the Holy Spirit, "Bend the stubborn heart and will; melt the frozen, warm the chill; guide the steps that go astray." It is through people filled with the Spirit that God's Church comes into being with the power of love to "renew the face of the earth."

Trinity Sunday

The prophets of the Old Testament are revered as people who communicated the word of God. Although these messages were not always welcome and the prophets suffered rejection and even death, time proved their wisdom and assured the veneration of their message.

The law was the other insight into the way to live as God's people. Moses, the great law-giver, handed on from God the basic guide to human life and happiness. The law, too, was distorted and ignored. For all of that, it was held in veneration as God's way. "Keep this law and commandments as I give them to you today so that you and your children may prosper and live long in the land the Lord your God gives you forever."

Moses put before his people the majesty of God and his special relationship to his people: "Was there ever a word so majestic, from one end of heaven to the other. ... Did ever a people hear the voice of the Living God speaking and remain alive?"

Everything that went before in the law and in the prophets was perfected in Jesus. Now the chosen people of God are all those who respond in love. "God does not have favorites." (Acts 10:34) The chosen land is all nations to whom the kingdom is to extend. The children of God know God as Father through the Divine Son who becomes their brother, united with them in the Holy Spirit whose life they share.

God, who is forever absolute, is revealed as Father, Son and Spirit dwelling in eternal love. God, in whose image we are created, is love. It is no wonder, then, that the whole law and prophets come to perfection in this expression of our destiny. That plan and destiny is that we become what we are made to be: the image of perfect love of Father, Son and Spirit. Jesus tells us the point to which all the law and the prophets was directed, "Love the Lord your God with all your heart ... love your neighbor as yourself." (Matthew 22:37–38) It has to be so if we are to be what we were created to be. God is love and we are the image of God.

Thus drawn into the life of God by union with Jesus and the life of the Holy Spirit, we have the courage to call God "Our Father." St Paul, the faithful preacher of Jesus, went further. The Spirit makes us God's children. Like Jesus we are even able to use the intimate, familiar, loving and trusting "Abba."

When Jesus revealed the intimate life of God he revealed God as absolute love. That is our eternal destiny. When we can really say "Abba, Father," with the depth of meaning that is the Spirit's gift, then we will be able to say and live with truth the words "brother" and "sister" to all of God's children. This is the fulfillment of the law and the prophets. This is the life of those who are one with the divine Son, giving praise by their lives to the Father in the love of the Holy Spirit.

The Body and Blood of Christ

"Christ has come as the high priest of all the blessings which were to come." Christ is the key to the fulfilment of everything possible to human nature. He is the source of all the riches and wisdom and knowledge, for it is "through him all things come to be." (John 1:3) More than this, he is the source of a life beyond the grasp of unaided human nature, even at its most brilliant heights. Christ is the source of the life of grace, God's own life, which can only be perfect gift from God. Through life in Christ we are lifted beyond that which is natural to that which is super-natural. "He brings a new covenant, as mediator, only so that the people who were called to an eternal inheritance may actually receive what was promised." By his death Jesus stood in our place so that we could rise with him to his place.

The wonder of the Eucharist is that we are able to make present in every place and time the sacrificial death by which we were redeemed, and the glorious resurrection which takes us to God. Christ's blood was drained from his body only once. He died and rose only once. But through the gift he made to us at the Last Supper we are privileged to make these realities present here and now and offer them to God. Thus we have access to an infinite treasure which is never diminished.

As we journey through life we are constantly renewed by tapping into the infinite riches of Christ. The life given us in Baptism and Confirmation is constantly renewed and strengthened in the Eucharist. We come to that constant flow of living water promised by Jesus to those who believe him.

However, it is a limited view of this wonder if it is seen solely as a private spiritual well. It is the offering of Jesus for all. Gathered around the ordained priest, the priestly people of God, here and now, present the sacrifice of Jesus to the Father. They remember the needs of all the living and they remember the dead. The community gathers as a priestly people given for all.

The Eucharist is both the cause of the community's gathering and the strength of the unity of those gathered. Thus we pray in the Mass and offer to the Father, "That we, who are nourished by his body and blood, may be filled with his Holy Spirit, and become on body, one spirit in Christ" (Third Eucharistic Prayer).

It is significant that the Eucharistic sacrifice is presented in the form of a meal. We invite our friends to join us in a meal, not because we believe they need something to eat, but to show gratitude, share ideas, joys, experiences, memories, concerns and life. We celebrate life together. Christ calls his followers to a life of unity and care for each other. He calls us to listen to his word and remember in his spirit to be ready to receive him in the most open way. For we are the bearers of his life to those not yet gathered around his Holy Table, and to each other.

Christ invites us to be guests at the holy table. Thank God we are here. Having accepted his invitation may we always enter into this holy exchange with minds ready to hear his word and wills ready to carry it out. May our hearts be waiting to be filled with the love only he can give. May our gratitude be expressed in eucharistic action, prayer, response and song.

Second Sunday of Ordinary Time

Observe the unselfish, courageous, gentle beauty to which we are called. The readings revealing today's message are full of unselfishness, courage, gentle encouragement and openness to the beauty of truth.

The call of God to Samuel is allowed to become clearer and finally specific by the understanding of Eli. The child Samuel is neither discouraged in his search nor is he given a presumptuous interpretation of his call. He is given a gentle response, time for understanding, and the encouragement to ask the right questions at the right time. God speaks and calls. Samuel listens. The wonder of their union takes place.

The beauty of unselfish human reaction is woven through these few lines of John's Gospel as well. John the Baptist looks long and hard, and knows. From love and knowledge he proclaims, "Look, there is the Lamb of God!" The first result is that two of his disciples leave him. Truth has already produced freedom, the search for deeper knowledge and the ultimate truth. They are free to go.

Jesus responds. They have followed him. He turns to them, encouraging them to continue their quest: "What do you want?"

"Rabbi, where do you live?" It is as though they are asking to be invited home. Jesus does just that and spends the rest of the day with them. It is all gentle encouragement. Here is no foot-in-the-door evangelization or conversion by the sword. It is invitation, exchange, dialogue. God is present to those who seek him. Truly here they are gathered in his name and he is among them.

As with John the Baptist, so with Andrew: true love can never be possessive, narrow or selfish. Andrew must also share his love and knowledge. Thus Simon Peter's figure is added to the picture as the kingdom grows so gently.

What wonders must have taken place in that little gathering of Jesus and his first disciples for Andrew to be able to declare without reservation or doubt, "We have found the Messiah." It was by sharing that wonder with his brother that Andrew brought Peter to Jesus. Peter is immediately loved and renamed by Jesus. He is God's man who will in time name Jesus as Christ, the Son of God.

God has a love and name for each of us. The disciples shared their faith and learnt their names. He invites us to discover this love and name by sharing our faith, hope and love with our fellow disciples as we journey together as his followers.

Third Sunday of Ordinary Time

"After John had been arrested, Jesus went to Galilee. There he proclaimed the Good News from God." It seems strange to say all that in two adjacent sentences. The man of goodness and truth is in prison, about to be beheaded by a selfish, petty ruler and there is good news from God.

It is a problem that people keep grappling with. Evil people get their way. The innocent suffer. Where is the good news from God?

This evil will invade the lives of Jesus and his disciples. Without contributing to it in any way and while striving, with every fiber of his being to overcome it, evil will attack and disturb Jesus. It will cause him deep sadness and suffering and a cruel death.

God's good news cannot be believed and realized without repentance. While selfishness prevails, suffering will be present. The preference of oneself for the hurt and destruction of another in any way blocks the flow of good news. Thus this opening statement of the mission of Jesus. A change is necessary if God's good news is to bring joy, happiness and full life to all. God's kingdom of justice, life and peace, of love and eternal life, is here. The only way hearts will be open to believing the Good News with real effect will be through repentance.

"Repent, and believe the Good News" is the plea of Jesus. While one remains turned inwards to self, excluding the dignity and respect that others deserve, there will be evil. The Kingdom will be here, its members at peace, but suffering. Jesus invites. Since God has made us free, he can do no more.

To this invitation we see the beautiful response of two sets of brothers. Reading the Gospel as a whole, we realize that much more than is recorded here has taken place in their interaction with Jesus and between themselves. Now they respond to the call to repent and believe. They leave the symbols of the past as any repentant person would do. They follow Jesus as every believer is called to do.

The disciples begin a journey to faith. There is yet much to change and much to learn before they, like Jesus, will be "fishers of men." But the risk has been taken, the journey begun.

It is important to realize that our own call to repent and believe goes on as theirs did. It is never just once and for all. It is important also to realize that it is not a journey of the feet or of places, but an interior journey. It is the journey that anyone can make and that all are called to make. If it requires changes of lifestyle or of place, so be it. But the call is to move inwardly to an ever greater realization of the wonder of God and the call of Jesus to follow him in his way of life. It is a call to be part of the prayer "Thy Kingdom come."

Fourth Sunday of Ordinary Time

As the people of Capernaum on the Northern shore of the sea of Galilee gathered in their synagogue on that sabbath to hear the scriptures and to pray, little did they know that they were about to hear the Word of God himself. And what a surprise it was when they did hear him. Joyful, exciting surprise made them wonder and listen. As Mark puts it, "His teaching made a deep impression on them." Drawing from the same writings as the scribes, he was outstandingly different from them. The writings were the same, the real source was vastly different.

These people in the Capernaum synagogue, like all the people of their land, had one law only and one lawgiver. There was no such thing as the separation of church and state. We are accustomed to think of the law of the Church and the law of the land. For them no such distinction existed. God was the lawgiver. They were God's people in the land God had given to them.

We experience the multiplication of laws in our society. Those with cunning and access to knowledge keep finding ways around existing laws. New laws are enacted to cover loopholes. In the time of Jesus, laws had multiplied and existed about all sorts of things. Besides this there were differing schools of thought among the scribes, Pharisees and lawyers. But the difference was that this was supposed to be God's law. In such a situation the reason for prescribing or proscribing some action could be forgotten in the maze of detailed interpretation that had been created. Remember, Jesus said that he had come, not to abolish the law but to bring it to perfection. He brought us back to essentials.

No wonder the people were surprised when they heard the beauty of God's mind expressed with conviction and clarity. Here was no scribe bogged down in trivial interpretations and petty disputes. Here was a call to experience the wonder of God and to a life befitting a people called God's chosen people.

The authority that surprised them came from the power of one who obviously was, and lived, the things he said. He spoke the word of God and was the Word of God. He could not be ignored. The evil present could not ignore him. In his turn he would not endure the evil spirits. The power of goodness spoke and the power of evil was dismissed.

Neither could the goodness within the people ignore him. "The people were so astonished that they started asking each other what it all meant. Here is a teaching that is new and with authority behind it." There seems always a thirst for goodness and for God. The sad thing is that so many things distract the seeker. We need renewal again and again in the spirit of excited children on a treasure hunt. Both "little children" and "hidden treasure" are the words of Jesus about the kingdom.

Fifth Sunday of Ordinary Time

"On leaving the synagogue" picks up from where we left off last Sunday. We saw Jesus go to the synagogue at Capernaum on the Sabbath and leave the people who came to worship with a feeling of wonder and awe in his presence.

It seems natural that he would go from the synagogue with his friends Simon and Andrew to their home. John and James go with them. However, if they expected a relaxed day they turned out to be quite mistaken. First, the hostess is sick, then the crowds, captivated by the events in the synagogue, begin to arrive and keep coming. (You notice they came in the evening, being good Jews, respecting the sabbath observance.)

The response of Jesus is his typical one. He sees, is moved to sympathy, and responds by caring action. We do not know how the crowds of people responded, but Simon's mother-in-law responded with gracious service. In his life Jesus is to experience forgetful ingratitude from some and warm, faithful gratitude from others. Here we see the second case exemplified. His healing calls us to willing and loving service.

But I believe that the sentence central to understanding this passage is, "In the morning, long before dawn, he got up and left the house and went off to a lonely place and prayed there."

Activity, even the loving activity of healing, is only temporary. The healing is important but it lasts only until the next time something comes to remind us that we are mortal. It is in silence with the Father that the deeper reality is perceived. Jesus is not merely the healer of mortal bodies but the bearer of an immortal gift.

If people were distracted from the reason for which he came, even by his healing powers, then he would leave that place and go to deepen the reality in the solitude of prayer. "Everybody is looking for you," say his friends. But why are they looking for him? How many have looked for Jesus as the answer to their problems and questions, only to leave disappointed because they have asked the wrong questions and sought things which have nothing to do with kingdom of God?

The heart of Jesus went out to the suffering, and he cured. But suffering and death returned. Death is part of life and the process to death is never pleasant. Jesus wants to give us something that will last. He wants to deliver us from the attitude of Job, "Swifter than a weaver's shuttle my days have passed, and vanished leaving no hope behind."

The gifts of the eternal Spirit of hope and wisdom are the real gifts of Jesus. Human life with all its comforts and blessings, hurts and ills, will remain much the same. It is the Spirit in which we live this life that will make the difference. Life with this Spirit has no end.

It is to preach with this Spirit and to offer this Spirit that Jesus moved from the comfort of acclamation to go to whatever reception he was to receive from people yet unknown.

Sixth Sunday of Ordinary Time

The man, clothing torn, hair disheveled, shielding his face as the law required—for he was a leper—pleads on his knees. From the dust he cries for help. With total faith in the power of Jesus the words are spoken, "If you want to, you can cure me." The faith, the words themselves, the condition of his brother, go straight to the compassionate heart of Jesus. The response is spontaneous, immediate, whole-hearted, "Of course I want you to be cured."

The wounded outcast with his cry of faith and hope brings to mind another such cry, yet to be uttered, from another reject: "Jesus, remember me when you come into your kingdom." There, too, was the immediate, overwhelming response, "Today you will be with me in paradise."

The fear of leprosy and the precautions of the law are understandable in the time and place they were given. But Jesus goes beyond human fear. Physical health and official cleanliness had come to be criteria for acceptability in the worshipping community, and even a sign of God's favor. Jesus declares that this is simply false.

Human societies of all times, including our own time, have in them that destructive element, dictated by those in power, that decrees who are acceptable and who unacceptable. Others are merely tolerated. Sometimes it is written into the law and is obvious. Ethnic cleansing is a disgusting example of this. In other cases the law forbids irrational discrimination, but it flourishes in the minds and hearts and in the speech and practices of people.

For Jesus there is no outcast, for his kingdom there is no outsider.

Jesus cut straight through this human nonsense. The light of the world pierced through the layers of prejudice to show us that here is a child of God. Those prejudices had created a caricature of him in the minds of others. His fellow human beings no longer saw a human person but a category, an object.

With the leper thus categorized and put in his place, the good clean people could go about their business. They would look after their own, do their work, make their way in life, pray to God. There was no need to go near lepers or be concerned about people like that. The law had put them in their place, and good people respected the law.

Jesus reached across the law. He touched the leper. For him the law had only one purpose. It was for our good. It was made for us, not us for it. If his attitude made him a leper in their minds, so be it. So he "had to stay outside in places where nobody lived."

Anyone who has stood by the outcast, the oppressed, the unacceptable in society, has had this experience. When we act on their behalf or speak up against ingrained prejudice or hatred or sustained bitterness, we risk being avoided and ignored. "I was treated like a leper" are words still understood today. Jesus understood them.

One person can make a difference. Jesus broke the taboo. "Even so, people from all round would come to him." He was not overwhelmed by institutionalized evil. He took steps. Others followed.

We rejoice in the fact that human history, in spite of its evils, records the lives of those who have taken the stance of Jesus, sometimes almost alone. Their fate has been the same as his. But we remember also that the cross was not really the end.

Seventh Sunday of Ordinary Time

Here is another Gospel example of the power of Jesus. I am not referring to his power to perform physical miracles or even the power to forgive sin as though these were something separate from the whole life of a person. I refer to his power to see as God sees. The outward appearance and state of life of the paralyzed man made him the one very obviously dependent on others. Some would say that his contribution to society was very minimal. His condition put him in a position of almost total dependence on others. He was weak, they were strong. He received, they gave. They were generous, he should be grateful.

So the power of Jesus to which I refer is the gift to see through the standards by which the world measures the worth of people. Here, the so called worthless one becomes the center of the scene. Again, it is through the weak, the little one, the dependent one, that we are able to see more clearly our own dependence on God and on each other.

The pride that prevents people from admitting this dependence would have caused this man to refuse help from his friends. To receive that help he first had to admit that he needed others. To receive healing he had to accept the facts as they were. This we call humility. Humility frees us to see things as they are. We need God. We need each other.

The humility which enabled the paralyzed man to accept his physical state and its consequences enabled him also to accept his sinful state. For, unless he had admitted the need for forgiveness and the spiritual growth and healing that forgiveness implies, he could not have been forgiven, even by God. Forgiveness, like love, to be effective, can never be only one way. What is given must be graciously received and lived out.

"Which is easier to say, 'your sins are forgiven,' or to say, 'Get up and walk?'"

The ethics of many religions and of many people with no religion have much in common. Christianity has to offer as a specific contribution these two virtues in today's Gospel: humility and forgiveness.

As the world progresses in scientific knowledge, but not in deep knowledge, understanding and acceptance of Christ's teaching, we realize that it is often easier to say, "get up and walk" than to say "you are forgiven." But even the cures that science offers are selective. The specifically Christian virtues are love that is not selective and care that is not limited to those we choose to call "our own."

When human beings are able to say to each other, across all barriers, "You are forgiven," and when we are able to admit the need for forgiveness and to accept it, then God's will to forgive will be liberated.

Perhaps then, in so many ways, to those lying in the degradation of hunger and disease, God will be able to say through Christ in us, "Get up and walk with dignity."

Eighth Sunday of Ordinary Time

"Do as you want," said to a mature, holy and loving person contains no risk whatever. The same words, said to the selfish or immature, are fraught with danger.

The new wine skins of which Jesus speaks today are the receptacles of his law of love. It is only those who are first renewed by unselfish love who can live with the new law of Jesus as their sole guide. For all the law and the prophets are summed up by Jesus in his command to love God undividedly and to love others as ourselves.

In the fresh skins of the hearts of those who want only what God wants—the new wine of the law of love—will rest easily. Any attempt to allow the immature and selfish to be guided by such a way of life will be disastrous. The trust of love will spill out into lust, oppression, greed or some expression of self-will.

The disciples of Jesus rejoice in the presence of the bridegroom and in the feast of God's and humanity's wedding in Jesus. They are being renewed and welcomed into the new law of love. It is a law that needs no words to tell them when and where and how to love their God and to love each other.

They will be given an ideal way of worship which will express all that the Savior is to do and to suffer. They will be called into a community of mutual service, expressing a unity that will cry out to the world that love is possible and that God is present through love's unselfish care.

Because the disciples of Jesus are loving people, their lives will be lives of concern and service for others. This implies effort, dedication, empathy and suffering more constant than set penance and times of fasting.

When the bridegroom is taken away they will be called on to endure a loss so much deeper than the loss of food for a day. As life goes on the bridegroom will come to them again only to depart in his physical presence. In the coming years there will be times of joy and consolation. There will be times of sorrow and desolation. Here is the fast of the followers of Jesus. He asks us to respond to the realities of life: to the needs of others, to the reality of our own condition of strength or weakness, to our own personality and state of health, to the wonderful things and the sorrowful things that come our way by our own design, the design of others or simply by accident.

As life unfolds it brings its own times of celebration and its penitential times. The disciple renewed in the spirit of Jesus is the new wine skin decanting the fresh wine of service in a freedom unknown to the person bound merely by law.

Ninth Sunday of Ordinary Time

The ten commandments were first announced to a people on a pilgrimage from slavery to freedom.

As Jesus tells us in today's Gospel, the law regarding the sabbath is for our freedom. It is so with all the commandments. God created us to live in freedom. It is necessary, therefore, to refrain from any activity that would unjustly restrict the freedom of others or inhibit our own growth to maturity. Thus the commandments.

The scribes and Pharisees had made a profession out of the interpretation of the law. The law had acquired an entity of its own as though it existed for itself. Jesus puts it into perspective. "The sabbath was made for man, not man for the sabbath."

We destroy the purpose of God's law when we extract the spirit. It is then seen merely as something to be done, a duty to fulfill before going on with life. The truth is that God's law is the key to life. When seen as merely duty the law becomes distorted. People begin to ask questions about the minimum required by the law. They ask how far they may go or how little they must do before sinning. People like the Pharisees are foolish enough to give answers. Thus the simple life-giving commandments, whose basis is love and freedom, become the subject of volumes filled with minute detail. Laws multiply as love diminishes.

"Observe the sabbath day and keep it holy" is part of the whole plan of God for our life as his free children. It is not a restriction of life but a necessary element for the development of life.

People deprived of work and its consequent self-expression and income also suffer from the effects of a maladjusted society. Likewise those whose whole life is centered on work, production and profit are deprived people. Notice that the commandment is set in that context. "For six days you shall labor and do all your work, but the seventh day is a sabbath for the Lord your God." The sabbath was created as a special day for celebrating life. Human beings are more than commodities at the disposal of the economy.

We need to stop on a regular basis, to think, to assess, to relate to family and friends in a deeper way, to be in touch with ourselves, our feelings and motives. We need to relate all that we do, think, work for, achieve and fail to achieve, and all that we are, to God. For God is the source of all and the ultimate end. We need to express our human and divine relationships. This rich variety of relationships and interdependence, as a gift from God, is expressed by worshipping together.

Our coming together to worship, our having time to share life, time to be rather than do, or even to do something different, are all why "the sabbath was made for man." The point is not what we do or refrain from doing, but taking time to develop genuine relationships with God and with each other.

The sabbath is a bit like work. Too much or too little can both be distortions. A sabbath ruled by laws creates tension and is seen as something to be endured is a distortion. Ignoring the sabbath, giving no recognition to God, the source of life and all creation, and having no time for others, is also a distortion of human life. Both are destructive.

With the priceless gift of the Eucharist inserted into our Christian sabbath, the Lord's day, the first day of the week, what a tragedy it is that this day is not treasured for the wealth of life it is meant to give.

Tenth Sunday of Ordinary Time

"How did your day go?" "Total confusion. Everyone seemed to want something, and all at the same time. I'm worn out." Have you ever received or given a reply like that?

When we say, "By the power of the Holy Spirit he became incarnate from the Virgin Mary and was made man," we are confessing belief in the fact that God stepped into our human confusion. Being human, the little things, the ordinary things, the aggravating people and circumstances, were part and parcel of the life of Jesus. The integrity and heroism he showed to an extraordinary degree in his final suffering and death were present during the whole of his life.

Today's Gospel passage shows Jesus in the midst of human confusion with some very aggravating people. God is not apart and aloof. He is with us.

By nationality Jesus is related to the people in that pressing crowd. By blood he is related to those who come to save him from himself. By official religion he is related to the scribes who come to condemn him.

What was meant to be a quiet meal at home, shared with a few friends, has turned into chaos. The crowd, probably seeking favors from the wonder-worker, shows little consideration in its self-seeking quest. The relatives interpret his generous response to the crowd and his zeal for God as madness. The scribes have committed a sin that can not be forgiven because they refuse to admit any need for change or forgiveness. They choose to be where they are and to stay there. To prove their case they even go to the extent of declaring publicly that Jesus is possessed by Satan. They are in the hopeless position of those who do not want to know the truth because they may not like what they hear. Even in the physical realm this is disastrous. People who will not consult the doctor because they may hear bad news cut themselves off from the help they may need. The scribes and those like them do the same in regard to conscience and the moral life. They block the Spirit of truth. God can not get near them to forgive.

Through all this confusion and sadness, Jesus keeps his focus on the one thing necessary. This he highlights when offered the temptation to give special attention to his closest relatives. Here is the opportunity to state again that it is not the flesh or anything the material world can give that will make the real difference to life. It is the Spirit. Close relationship with Jesus is in direct proportion to our response to God's will. It depends on love. "Anyone who does the will of God, that person is my brother and sister and mother."

Through the chaos of accusation of madness, striving for favors and position, even the awful accusation that Satan is in this beautiful person, Jesus still gives clear direction to his disciples. God's way may seem mad to the greedy and ambitious; in fact it is the only way to wholeness, sane relationships and happiness.

Eleventh Sunday
of Ordinary Time

Reflecting on the parables of the kingdom of God, what comes to mind? Is it the growth of the Church from the small, almost invisible beginning to its present wide spread? Do we regret that, in many places, the prestige and position of power and influence that the Church once seemed to have are somewhat diminished? Do we rejoice, however, that the Pope still commands respect and receives attention and acclaim wherever he goes?

Today, allow Jesus to speak to you personally in these parables. The kingdom of God is within you. Within each of us the priceless seed has been sown. It is of inestimable value, for it is the presence of God himself. The seed that died so that life might flourish in us is Jesus. He is planted in the earth in our human nature. The life that springs from that unseen seed is the life of the Spirit of God, who is now one with us. It is the will of the Eternal King that what he has planted will grow to maturity and bear a rich harvest itself.

Consider, then, the way in which this sacred seed produced his harvest. Only when Jesus was buried in the ground did the kingdom flourish in the hearts of the believers. The beauty of a death that leads to life was seen in the resurrection. His kingdom came by his unselfish service, by total dedication to God's way. When he had accomplished all he had to do, he was ready to go. Having gone, the Holy Spirit realized the kingdom in the hearts of his followers. Here is the model of the kingdom.

It is a kingdom far removed from a Church of material or physical power. Are the times and places of high political power, high prestige and material strength, the times when the Church has been outstanding in its imitation of the suffering servant of God? The kingdom is realized through unselfish service, humble forgiveness and universal love. The kingdom comes when the Church is not only the Church for the poor, but the Church of the poor.

Jesus knows how easily we misunderstand the things of the Spirit. He seems to struggle here to find an image through which we can understand. "What can we say the kingdom of God is like?" Even then he will be misunderstood, so "He would not speak to them except in parables." He did not want to give further excuse for their misunderstanding. If they were serious they would come closer and eventually see the real meaning of life; "But he explained everything to his disciples when they were alone."

In the parable of the mustard seed we also see the kingdom as service. It is there not to dominate by its size and strength, but to receive all who would seek refreshment in its all-embracing branches. It is there to serve. Here there are no elite favorites. The arms of love reach out to all as the branches of the tree are ever ready, waiting to offer the weary bird leafy refreshment.

Twelfth Sunday of Ordinary Time

If we are in the same boat as Jesus, sometimes it will be a frightening experience, sometimes an experience of peace and calm.

The invitation is there for the disciples, "Let us cross to the other side." That invitation continued to be extended to the new disciples after Pentecost. It is extended to us, the disciples of today. It is Jesus who takes the initiative and issues the invitation to all. He awaits our acceptance.

In the invitation to cross to the other side he is asking them to set out for the eastern bank of the Sea of Galilee. He invites them into pagan territory. Here is a journey with risk enough. It is to be undertaken by the Church in the time of Mark. The people of Mark's time knew the hazards involved in crossing from the familiar territory of their people into pagan territory. We, too, are invited to move with Jesus. We are invited to take him into our land of disbelief and doubt.

Mark will also know that taking Jesus aboard will mean going out into the deep by leaving behind traditions and practices no longer compatible with a new way of life. Some things have to be left behind. This, too, is an invitation to all disciples. What is incompatible with life in the same boat as Jesus must be jettisoned. This involves the storm.

In taking Jesus on board we launch into the supernatural life. Jesus is in his Church, the assembled people of God. He is in each member of his people. God's life, God's mind, God's will are expressed to the world in this way through the continuing presence of Jesus. Thus we launch into the deep, carrying Jesus with us. Heading for the other side, we have the troubled seas to contend with, for the Spirit of Jesus is not compatible with the spirit of the world.

The disciples felt the absence of the power of Jesus in the boat on troubled seas. They experienced the feeling of being helpless when the force opposing them persecuted them and killed them. When we are faithful we sometimes share this feeling of standing alone. This is why Mark asks the early Christians and us to remember that, in times of trouble, Jesus is there. He does care. He will take control. He will see us through and save us. When he slept in the boat he was still present. When he slept in death they seemed alone and forgotten. He was with them all through and stilled the storm of fear and doubt in the resurrection.

In our time, faithfulness to God by constant prayer, striving for honesty and justice, working and longing for a Church which expresses on every level, the loving, forgiving, welcoming presence of Jesus, we may feel alone. We are not. Jesus may seem to be asleep. He is with us in the troubled waters and is seeing us through to the other side. While the boat makes its journey he is still the one to give us the blessing of his peace, all the while calling for the depth of faith that overcomes all.

Thirteenth Sunday of Ordinary Time

We don't know the answer to why a little girl should die at twelve years of age, or why a woman should suffer for twelve years. The child's whole life was as long as the time the woman had lived with this debilitating illness. We can't find a reason for either.

According to the Book of Wisdom, it is all tied up with evil. "Death was not God's doing, he takes no pleasure in the extinction of the living … it is the devil's envy that brought death into the world. …"

It is possible to trace the connection between suffering and sin in the evils we bring upon ourselves. It is certain that God does not want us to be murderers, drunken drivers, rapists, cheats or deceptive in our relationships. He does not want people with power to use it unjustly. He does not want systems whereby some live in luxury and others starve; or evil political systems or organized crime. God does not want us to fight and kill each other. It is easy to see the cause and effect between these things that God forbids and their evil outcome of human suffering, even for the innocent.

It is not so easy to see the connection between sin and the suffering of people like those in today's Gospel. Their suffering relates to our mortality. Since we are going to die we go through a process of dying. Why it should be an early death for some and old age for others, or little suffering for some and much for others, is a mystery.

What today's Gospel tells us is that the mystery does not consist in the fact that God has abandoned us to our own devices and turned the other way. Here God spells out, in the actions of his Word, that he is right in the midst of it all.

Jesus cured only a few people and brought back to life fewer still. But they are representative of all. Did you ever consider the range of people: young and old, male and female, that Jesus touched, spoke to and called to a fuller life? Children, women, men, young, old, Jewish, gentile, innocent, sinful, with ailments ranging from skin diseases through to death. Some asked for themselves; others had loved ones to ask for them. Here is life, suffering, human relationships, healing, joy, relief, gratitude, love, faith, prayer—all that is life.

Jesus cured, but yet the people died in the end. In his intervention he gave us more than bodily healing. He called each one to the new life of greater faith. He offers something more lasting. He offers a way of living, loving and believing that will be the source of peace and happiness through all of life's contingencies. He assures us that human life does matter. We are reminded in the first reading that we are God's image. What really makes the difference in the lives of the people of today's Gospel is what makes the difference in any life—faith.

Jesus makes a distinction between the people physically close to him and the one who is close in faith. This one touched his power. That power, then, was able to touch her.

Suffering, sickness, everything in life—even sin—can be a place from which we can go forward into fuller life and deeper faith. He is ever calling us to the peace and freedom he gave to the one here he called "my daughter."

Fourteenth Sunday of Ordinary Time

"They were astonished when they heard him," is said of Jesus more than once in the Gospels. "Where did this man get all this?" is surely the right question. But these people did not wait for an answer. They heard wisdom such as they had never heard before, and saw works that they could only describe as miracles. Then the blockage came. It is the same barrier that prevents so much good from being done, so much wisdom from being absorbed and the spreading of understanding among human beings. They categorized Jesus.

It is not the goodness of God or the saving power of Christ that is wanting for the solution of our human problems. The narrow and closed minds of people prevent the truth from penetrating the darkness. The significance of these words is important, "he could work no miracle there. … He was amazed at their lack of faith."

God can not go back on his word. He created us in his own likeness so that we are able to love. The freedom to love will not be taken away even when we abuse it. If we choose not to respond in love and hope to God and creation, then he can work no miracle in us or through us.

"This is the carpenter, surely, the son of Mary. …" When we realize what sort of place Nazareth was we will know what they meant. When Philip told Nathanael about Jesus of Nazareth his immediate response was, "Can anything good come from Nazareth?" It certainly was not the place of origin for prophets and kings.

The difference between Nathanael and the people in this Gospel passage is that Philip's invitation to "Come, see for yourself," was taken up by Nathanael. He saw, he listened, he changed direction. Nathanael's life took off on its wonderful journey with Jesus.

The Gospels are written for us and about us. Jesus is both the message and the redeeming power of God for us. He is also one of us. He is in us moving towards God. This is true of all who carry his Spirit within them. We take this message to the world and at the same time are ourselves taken by the message into the life of God.

Now if we apply that to today's Gospel, do we say of ourselves, "This is only ... from ..." or do we really believe in the presence and power of God within?

Or, do we put others into a safe category where we need take no notice of them? If we do these things we behave like the people of Nazareth. We hope for nothing, rather than looking in joyful expectation as we go along the road with Jesus.

It is an insult to God to put people into categories as though they were mere things. Each is the result of the creative mind of God. May we never insult God by saying, "What more could you expect from a ...?" The "..." is usually race, religion, sex, age or some other category with which some human being has been labeled and limited.

Fifteenth Sunday of Ordinary Time

During the time Jesus spent with his disciples he often spoke of things to come. The kingdom would come in its own way, in its own time. In today's Gospel incident, Jesus, by his actions, foreshadowed things to come. In the end, which would be the beginning, he would send them out with his own authority to teach all nations. Here he gives a hint of that great act of trust he will make in his followers, in his Church. He calls them together as a body, sends them on a limited mission. They go, not as individuals with their own skills and ideas to promote, but in pairs, representing the gathering to which they have been summoned. They go out together, having received authority from Jesus. "Jesus summoned the twelve and began to send them out in pairs, giving them authority over unclean spirits."

Last week we reflected on those people who saw Jesus as merely the carpenter, the son of Mary. The result was, "He could work no miracle there." In contrast, the disciples gathered in faith, ready to receive the power that came from him.

If anyone is to be a force against the evil that Jesus is to overcome, that person must be open to receive power from Jesus. The disciples were ready to receive. They believed in the power of Jesus. Their faith had opened them to God's power.

This faith is not merely an absence of doubt. It consists in a thorough trust that makes the disciple free from all that blocks the channels of God's power. Disciples are told to leave behind all excess baggage. Their concern is to be instruments of the liberating power of Jesus. God will take care of the rest. If they cannot trust Jesus in this, how can they say they have faith? Those who are to bring others freedom from evil must first be on the road to freedom themselves.

This freedom is not just a freedom from undue anxiety about the needs of the body. It is also a freedom from pride and the lure of self importance. Jesus warns the disciples of the failure and frustration he has experienced. He is not there to be acclaimed as king but to do the will of the Father. In the same way they are to take God's message. There are those who will welcome it with love and those who will reject it. Their mission is to offer God's love, not to impose their own will. They are not sent for personal success or achievement but for the kingdom of love and freedom. "And if any place does not welcome you and people refuse to listen to you ... walk away."

As with the prophet Amos before them, so with the disciples, it was not their idea that they be called. It was God's choice. It was theirs to be faithful to the call. In the eyes of proud people, Amos, the apostles, Jesus himself, did not rate highly on the financial or social scale. Their power was from God and for others. It is this unselfish use of power for good to which all followers of Jesus are called and committed.

Sixteenth Sunday of Ordinary Time

Jeremiah laments over the lost opportunity and wasted gifts of those empowered by God to lead his people to goodness. He also says that, although human beings betray God's trust, God will not abandon us.

"The Lord is my shepherd." This is true. How he is my shepherd is revealed in the scriptures. We are assured that his goodness and kindness are his gifts to us all the days of our lives. This goodness and kindness he places in the hearts of his creatures to grow by their being given to others. Their final expression is the rapture of God's direct love.

It is in the Gospel that we see this happening. Remember last week's reflection on the sending out of the disciples to be dispensers of the goodness and kindness of the Lord? Jesus sent them out two by two. Now they come back to share with him the joy they received in giving what they had received. All of this needed to be reflected upon. "You must come away to some lonely place. ..." There had been a time for teaching and for activity. Now was the time for reflective prayer, seeing where God was in all of this and acknowledging his powerful presence so that it would be confirmed in them.

Activity without reflection can become automatic and sterile. Jesus knew this.

We would like to think that if Jesus had planned a time of rest and retreat that it would be sure to happen. Here we are brought down to earth again. Jesus is one of us and had to contend with unexpected circumstances. We plan good things and something comes up to disrupt the plan. As with our plans, so with his, it is mostly the call of other needs that gets in the way.

What comes first? This is the dilemma of Jesus here. It is a question common to good people. As we mature and grow in goodness there will still be the occasional temptation, the choice between good and evil. Even Jesus was tempted. But the most common choices for good people are those between things that are good and that which is best. Discerning the best if not always easy. Should Jesus and his disciples go ahead and spend generous time with God in a lonely place, or spend time with people who need the presence of God in the flesh of Jesus and his disciples? The circumstances help them to choose the latter.

The end result was the same, it seems. "He set himself to teach them at some length." This could have happened in the quiet of the "lonely place." But for Jesus and those close to him every place is the place of God's presence. Every person has something to hear from us, and something to say to us, of the presence of God.

We are all both the sheep who need the refreshing pastures and the shepherds who provide those pastures. What we do need is prayerful reflection so that we see this and make deliberate choices for good. Reflect here and now and choose to enter into this act of worship with deliberate intention and attention.

Action after reflection and reflection after action make for wise decisions by which to live. Deciding what is best is sometimes obvious but often very difficult. The Lord is my shepherd in prayerful thought, accurate information and wise and good friends. Thus he guides me along the right path.

Seventeenth Sunday of Ordinary Time

In the Sunday Masses of year B the Gospel readings work through the Gospel of Mark. At this point we have come to the place in that Gospel where Mark records the miracle of the loaves and fish. This is one incident which is recorded in all four Gospels.

However, this morning's reading is not from Mark's Gospel. For five weeks we switch to John's Gospel and to his account of this miracle. The sixth chapter of John's Gospel develops this story from the life of Jesus in a much fuller way than the other evangelists do. John draws conclusions from it that are rich with implications for the Church of his time and for all times. The liturgy makes full use of this wonderful gift in the holy scriptures.

In today's section of that sixth chapter of John's Gospel we see the actual miracle related and allusions to the meanings that will become clearer as the story unfolds.

People are fascinated by the mysterious and unusual. Here we see people so fascinated by Jesus and his healing and teaching that they follow him and are so caught up that they neglect the necessities of life. They are out there without food.

Through this need itself, God's presence can be further appreciated. Need can lead to frustration or inventiveness, to despair or hope, to selfishness or sharing of resources. Positive results can come from negative circumstances. We can also learn about our own need for others and our power for others, our weakness and our strength.

This is just what happens here. Jesus does not criticize the people because they came in response to the wonders they saw. He takes them as they are and calls them to further knowledge and true faith. First, the apostles are asked to share in solving the problem. The question of Jesus to Philip, "Where can we buy some bread for these people to eat?" calls him into sharing the situation. Then Andrew and Philip seem to invite Jesus to respond to their inventiveness and to the generosity of the small boy. The process has begun. By trustful sharing, the wall of isolation that creates need begins to crumble.

In the face of world problems and even of problems close to home, our response can be a question like, "What are these among so many?" when we think of any effort we might make towards solving the problem. The little boy's contribution seemed trivial. It was the beginning, the specific act of generosity that brought about the solution. Who knows the end result of a word or act that begins a process of forgiveness or understanding? Who knows the end result of an unselfish, humble act of kindness, a word of encouragement or praise or thanks? Who knows the benefit of a gift given in joy to the needy?

The crowd is fed and there is more than enough.

Unfortunately, the message is misunderstood. Rather than listening to Jesus, the crowds want Jesus to listen to them. God has done them a favor. They need a powerful king. God would have to be blind not to see it their way. This is the king to get us on top of the world again.

The way of Jesus is otherwise. It is what has just happened. In trust they shared their anxieties, hopes, food, time. Each gave what each had to give and left the rest to God.

When we pray "Thy kingdom come," we commit our-
selves to contributing our part, letting others contribute theirs,
and leaving the rest to God.

Eighteenth Sunday of Ordinary Time

After the miracle of the loaves and fish, "Jesus escaped back to the hills by himself," (John 6:15) to avoid the misdirected enthusiasm of the crowd. The people wanted this man of power to be their man of power, their leader. Power which could satisfy the hunger of thousands could be harnessed for their cause.

If these people thought that food without work was a great opening to an election campaign for national leadership, they were wrong.

Yes, they had gone to a lot of trouble to find Jesus after the miracle and to be with him. But he asks why. He did not come to gather thousands, millions of followers just for the sake of numbers. Thoughts like, "we are the largest religion in the world" or "Jesus should be grateful that I am here at all," are challenged. Why do they seek him?

Jesus contrasts two interpretations of the miracle and its purpose. He contracts two interpretations of life. First, "You are looking for me ... because you had all the bread you wanted to eat," secondly, "Work for the food that endures to eternal life." Human beings are more than their animal component, sustained by food. Life is more than mere survival. Obviously, bodily sustenance is vital to life on earth. After all, Jesus had just been concerned that the people were hungry and did something about it. But full human life, and even food for all, involves the will and the spirit behind the human will.

The distribution of the fruits of the earth, the use of nuclear energy, the purposes to which the wonders of modern communications and mass media are directed, all depend on the unseen powers in all of us.

It is not what we possess or produce as individuals or as a nation or a world, but the spirit that gives direction to these things, that makes the difference. We can use these powers to destroy or to create. Full life involves love, thought, creativeness, prayer, sharing, community. It is of body, mind, heart and soul. Through Jesus, God enters our life and lifts it into his own eternal life.

Thus, when asked the question, "What must we do if we are to do the work that God wants?" Jesus answered, "This is working for God: you must believe in the one he has sent." Believing in Jesus implies accepting the fact that his teachings will work. It implies the risk of being truly Christian: one who does not cling, but shares life and all that creates free spirits filled with God's Spirit, knowing God loves all.

Material wealth and abundance of resources will never make the difference. The world has the resources. It is the spirit of the world or the Spirit of God in people that will free the captives of poverty, war, hatred and want.

It is not bread that is wanting, but the Spirit who will give life to the bread and to those who share it. This is "the kind of food the Son of Man is offering you."

Nineteenth Sunday of Ordinary Time

"No one can come to me unless drawn by the Father who sent me." Life, full human life and eternal life are God's gifts. All we have to do is to accept what God offers through the one he has sent. He is the one through whom all the things of life were made and the one who will raise us up on the last day to eternal life.

We need to take prayer seriously so that we are in touch with the gifts within us and around us and in touch with God who is in us and around us. Gratitude for these gifts, temporal and eternal, will draw us into deeper union with God. Then, being "taught by God," we will come to Jesus and live like Jesus.

It is so important to listen and reflect. God made the sublime gift of his Son to humanity. Jesus accepted all that this implied, all that we are and do, except sin, so that we could be one with him. He ate the bread of our human life so that we could eat the bread of divine life. Yet it was the very ordinariness of this, the humility of his act of self-abasement, the humanness of his life, that made it too close to see. "Surely this is Jesus, son of Joseph. We know his father and mother. How can he say, 'I have come down from heaven?'" We must pray and listen so that we, too, do not miss the point through over-familiarity.

Jesus gives his followers an extraordinary way of staying in touch. He contrasts the bread that satisfies the body with the bread that leads to eternal life. He is that bread which sustains spiritual power, and brings real meaning to life and direction and purpose to the use of all talents and material gifts. He has shown us in the miracle how life works when we listen to even the least (the little boy) and share even the smallest gifts (the few loaves and fish). All wisdom and knowledge are his. He is the source of full life here and hereafter.

We need to stay in touch with this, to stay in touch with Jesus. It is in this context that Jesus reveals the extraordinary gift that enables his followers to be with him and to grow in his life. He will be their bread of real life. When we eat ordinary bread it sustains our life at it is absorbed by our bodies. So he will be the food we absorb into our being to sustain and increase his life within us. Since Jesus is God, eternal with the Father and the Holy Spirit, his life, in whomever it is, can never die. It must be raised up as he was raised up by the Father.

God's being and our being are in a holy communion with each other. It follows that we live the kind of life that Christ lived, expressing the God who is one with his child.

All that John wrote here was written to a Church, a people who already shared the bread of life and the cup of salvation around the table of the Lord. To them and to us his meaning is obvious. When we receive the Holy Eucharist we receive the one who came down from heaven to give life to the world. We receive Jesus who tells us, "My flesh is real food, my blood is real drink."

May we never forget the wonder of this gift through closeness, its ready availability, or familiarity with humble signs of bread, wine and human words. Filled with wonder, awe, gratitude and love, let us approach the table of the Lord with confidence and trust in his welcome to all who come to him. Let his life of unselfish love be lived again through us, since we are one body, one spirit, with and through him.

Twentieth Sunday of Ordinary Time

"I am the living bread come down from heaven. Anyone who eats this bread will live for ever; and the bread that I shall give is my flesh, for the life of the world."

It is not usual for the readings of the liturgy to be repeated on successive Sundays. The above verse is repeated. The final verse of last Sunday's Gospel is the first verse of today's.

Those words are the climax of the sixth chapter of John's Gospel. Beginning with the miracle of the bread for the thousands, John records Jesus introducing his followers to the climax of the whole Gospel. Jesus is from heaven, one in life with the Father. He is human life which can be given, poured out, spent. He pours out his life in service and finally in sacrificial offering, not only that thousands may have bread, but that all may have eternal life. His life is bread and wine given for the life of the world. He invites us to be one flesh and one blood with him so that by eating this bread and drinking this wine we will draw life from him. Our life, then, as his, will be life in union with God. It will be life poured out in loving service of others in fidelity to God, and then eternal life with the father.

In their accounts of the Last Supper, Matthew, Mark and Luke tell us of Jesus giving his disciples the bread that is his body, the wine that is his blood. Each recalls that these are given and poured out for all. St Paul, too, writing to the christians in Corinth, reminds them that the Eucharistic gathering is a re-presenting, a showing forth, of the death of the Lord. All four use the language of sacrifice. The Lord offers himself, pours out life for us.

John, in his Last Supper presentation tells of Jesus laying down his life for us. He presents Jesus divesting himself and going down to wash the disciples' feet.

It is in this sixth chapter of his Gospel that John recalls the other elements of the Last Supper. Here is Jesus giving us bread and wine, broken and poured out, drawing all to himself, given to us for the life of the world.

These central themes of the Gospel can not be separated without distorting the message. The final laying down of his life is one with the constant laying down of life in feeding the hungry or washing the feet of the disciples. All are life poured out in service to others and fidelity to the God of truth and the truth of God.

The offering of Jesus in the Eucharist is the re-presenting of this life and death offered to the Father and taken into our being as the bread of this kind of life. Those who eat his flesh and drink his bood are one with all of this. "… whoever eats me draws life from me." Union with Jesus in receiving his body and blood implies union with his service to others and his fidelity to the Father. It implies union with his heart, mind, teaching and attitudes towards God and towards all.

Twenty-first Sunday of Ordinary Time

"This is intolerable language. How could anyone accept it?" There it was in the beginning, even as Jesus was establishing his Church and giving it the sign of his constant love and the sign and cause of its unity. It has gone on ever since, and today someone, somewhere, is surely saying, "How could anyone accept it?"

The truths that Jesus revealed here about God, about the Eucharist and about our final destiny are not self-evident. If they were, they would need no revelation. The truth that Jesus asks the people to accept, as recorded here, is far from self-evident. Thus they ask, "How can this man give us his flesh to eat?" (Last Sunday's Gospel.)

No bodily sense can inform us that Christ is present in the Eucharist and that in this act of worship we present Christ's sacrifice to the Father. Sight, sound, smell, touch, taste, tell us nothing about the Holy Trinity, the power of the sacraments or the life of heaven.

This is the point that Jesus makes here, "It is the Spirit that gives life, the flesh has nothing to offer. The words I have spoken to you are spirit and they are life." First, it all depends on God's gift. "This is why I told you that no one could come to me unless the Father allows him." Secondly, it depends on our attitude to that gift. "What about you?" asks Jesus.

Does the disciple accept Jesus as the one, "come down from heaven ... for the life of the world?" If the answer is yes, then all falls into place. Then Jesus speaks with an authority which cannot be doubted. God speaks. All his words are for the "life of the world." We are not able to grasp the full meaning or imagine how it can be, but since it is God who speaks, it has to be so. This, too, is why, since divine faith concerns God's revelation, no human authority whatever may add to it, diminish it, or bind another to accept a theological or philosophical opinion or a mere human interpretation of it.

Thus the response of Peter was, "Lord whom shall we go to? You have the message of eternal life, and we believe, we know that you are the Holy One of God." What is revealed is beyond the senses and beyond the imagination; even beyond, but not contrary to reason. But the act of faith is founded on the knowledge that God spoke through Jesus. The disciples discovered this through the life and teaching of Jesus, which were totally authentic, and through his fidelity in death and the vindication of all in his resurrection. We, too, have, by the grace of God, come to know the truth of the one who is Word of God. For the same reasons that impelled the apostles, we, too, look to Jesus with absolute faith and confidence.

Faith goes further than the senses or reason, but its foundation, the authenticity of Jesus, is eminently reasonable. Faith is more than mere belief. It is that yes to God through Jesus, in the Spirit, to his gift. It is a total response to God, of mind, will and soul, impelling us to Christian belief, action and prayer.

In the confusion of life we need to call upon the Spirit continually. The flesh, even the flesh of Jesus, profits us nothing without communion in and with his Spirit. The apostles open their hearts to the Spirit and when "they see the Son of Man ascend to where he was before," that Spirit is poured upon them. Like the apostles, we are not perfect when offered the flesh of the Son of Man, but those who long for the truth from his Spirit are filled with that Spirit. Then with strength, courage and love, faith leads to prayer, and prayer leads to action for truth and love.

Twenty-second Sunday of Ordinary Time

Jesus condemns religion which makes people feel good by performing some religious act while they use, despise or even kill others. His message to these Pharisees and scribes is as appropriate today as it was when first delivered. He is not speaking in these harsh terms to people who, while striving to love God and others, fail through human weakness. These he loves, forgives and encourages to get up and walk with him again.

Those whose hearts are fixed on loving God and all others may sometimes fall short of this high ideal. But they will know when they fail, experience sorrow, and seek forgiveness.

There is a world of difference between the humble, imperfect Christian idealist and the proud, self-seeking fanatic. Whether the fanaticism is fixed on race, nation, religion or self-promotion, the "cause" will become more important than people. It will usually be backed by slogans and have its symbols. We know the slogans under which people have suffered and still suffer: purity of race, ethnic cleansing, superior person, upper class, higher caste and terms such as "little more than an animal." From such lack of respect or self aggrandizement, "fornication, theft, indecency, envy, slander, pride, folly," will surely follow.

Jesus names our relationship with God as a matter of the heart. He has said it elsewhere, "Where your treasure is, there will your heart be also." (Matthew 6:21) The way we regard God and God's creation, the esteem we have for the work of his hand, the love we have for him, will determine our attitude. Then our attitude will give rise to our words and actions. "Pure unspoiled religion" is firstly a matter of the heart. It concerns what we want, based on what we believe and accept and love. It is from this core, this center, this heart of our being that desires and then actions proceed.

"Nothing that goes into a man from outside can make him unclean; it is the things that come out of a man that make him unclean." Empty ritual from unclean hearts only compounds the evil because it makes the wrong-doer feel justified.

Love, the first commandment of Jesus, stands. From this all else follows. A Christian who is really a follower of Christ in spirit and in truth could never feel justified by mere external acts or by empty words acclaiming loyalty. From a God-centered heart, God-like deeds will follow.

All of the commandments are about right relationships with God, with others, within ourselves and towards creation. True, unspoiled religion flows from the reality of things as they are, is integrated with life, is creative and leads to freedom. This freedom concerns the rights and duties of all and will flourish only through respect for all. It will produce a people about whom it can be said, "No other people is as wise as this great nation."

Twenty-third Sunday of Ordinary Time

Last week we saw Jesus with the representatives of religious authority and law, the Pharisees and scribes. Here he is with outcasts in the pagan area of Tyre and Sidon and the Decapolis region. Yet there is a sad contrast. The Pharisees and scribes come with questions about their precious customs. These outsiders bring a fellow human being in need. The Pharisees and scribes are inward-looking, self-defensive and critical of change. They see the words of man-made laws rather than God's law with the care for others it implies. Concentrating on their own religious customs, they are unconcerned about the damage done by ignoring God's own law while enforcing these customs.

The prophet Isaiah gives signs of the presence of God among his people. He tells of the glorious times when that presence will reach its peak, because it is recognized. "Then the eyes of the blind shall be opened, the ears of the deaf unsealed, then the lame shall leap like the deer and the tongues of the dumb sing for joy." God's judgment is a judgment that puts things right. When John the Baptist's followers asked if Jesus was the one to come, his answer was a reference to this passage of scripture.

The restoration of creation goes deeper than these outward signs. The healing of the human race implies more than perfect human bodies. If everyone on earth at this moment became a perfect physical specimen, but without change of mind or conversion of heart, not a day would pass before we again had made each other blind and lame and deaf. Jesus offers more than physical healing and calls for more than cures by miracles of God or of modern science.

The contrast drawn between the Pharisees and scribes last week and the pagans of today is between knowledge, law and closed minds, and the gifts of human compassion, a searching attitude for truth and a willingness to listen and learn. Both groups ask something: the first, not to learn but to make a point of their own; the second, in the hope of finding a solution to their present distress, and perhaps, to greater, more lasting realities.

Hearing is a precious gift. The man in the story was indeed favored. Anything we can do to improve the hearing of those affected by deafness or to facilitate communication should be done. But Jesus knows that hearing is only part of receiving his message or the message of anyone. Whether people are deaf or possessed of perfect hearing will tell us nothing about their willingness to understand or their capacity to interact and change where necessary.

We Christians are called to be leaders in developing the practice of effective listening. Only by letting Jesus touch our ears and our tongues with his gifts of understanding, compassion, forgiveness and genuine loving concern, can we begin to stop and ask ourselves, "What am I hearing, what meaning lies behind these words, what meaning am I conveying to the other?"

When we come to pray the "Our Father" today, stop and ask, "What did I just commit myself to by saying those words?" If we do this often, perhaps Jesus will touch our ears and our tongues to enable them to really hear his words and the words of others and to proclaim his praise through life-giving words like his.

Twenty-fourth Sunday of Ordinary Time

The things Jesus said and the way he lived made him appear to people like, "John the Baptist, Elijah or one of the prophets." At least those people were perceptive enough to see that here was a man of God, a chosen messenger of the truth, a fearless, special person.

From his privileged vantage point and by the gift of God's enlightenment, Peter was able to go further. He had come to the conclusion that here in front of him was the final prophet, the anointed of God, the Christ. "You are the Christ," is the response to the vital question. Jesus acknowledged this fact but indicated that the time was not right for its promulgation. The people would not yet understand what it meant to be the Christ. "He gave them strict orders not to tell anyone about him." There would come the proper time for that.

So Jesus began to let this little band of disciples know that being the Christ meant, "to suffer grievously, to be rejected by the elders and chief priests and the scribes and to be put to death. ..." Perhaps Peter was so overwhelmed by these awful words that he did not even hear the phrase "and after three days to rise again." He would not be the last disciple to be overwhelmed by the things that go before rising again with Christ.

Probably the best work Satan can do is to have someone acknowledge the Christ, preach the Christ, show loyalty to the

Christ, but be totally wrong about what it means to be the Christ. By rejecting God's way of being the Christ, Peter is creating a false Christ, not in God's image, but in his own image. Thus the harsh words, "Get behind me Satan! Because the way you think is not God's way but man's."

It is still legitimate for Jesus to ask his followers or those who use his name as Christians, "Who do you say I am?" Is he the Savior who delivers us from trouble, keeps us safe and successful, gets us a job, makes sure we pass examinations, keeps poverty and the poor at a distance, fights with our armies, conquers enemies and makes sure we are comfortable?

In a way the answer given by the people who said, "John the Baptist or one of the prophets," was a better answer than Peter's. John the Baptist and the prophets, like Jesus, all got into trouble or were exiled, imprisoned or killed for the truth, justice and for preaching God's way. The reason was not a perverse desire by God to see them suffer, but the perversity and selfishness of people who refused to face the truth. Facing the truth implies change, risk and the chance of losing something for the sake of others and for eternal life.

There is only one way of being his disciple, and that is by preferring justice and love even more than life. Has he not told us that those who want to be his followers must renounce themselves, take up their cross and follow him? Embracing those things that lead to the redemption of the world means embracing unselfish prayer, work, causes, ideals. It means working for a political way and for a Church, too, which are less concerned with preserving what they hold than with taking a risk for the sake of fuller life for all. "For anyone (including ourself, our country, our Church) who wants to save his life will lose it, but anyone who loses his life for my sake, and for the sake of the Gospel, will save it." Jesus still asks, "Who do people say I am?" The answer goes beyond mere words.

Twenty-fifth
Sunday
of Ordinary Time

It is a week since we read in the Sunday liturgy, "He began to teach them that the Son of Man was destined to suffer grievously, to be rejected by the elders and the chief priests and scribes and to be put to death, and after three days to rise again." Today once more, Jesus tells his disciples, "The Son of Man will be delivered into the hands of men; they will put him to death, and three days after he has been put to death he will rise again." Obviously it was a difficult message for the disciples to comprehend and to accept. Mark tells us that six days after Jesus made the first of these two predictions of his death and resurrection, the transfiguration took place and they saw his glory. He then healed the young man possessed by the deaf and dumb spirit that hurled him into the fire and water. This is why today's Gospel begins, "After leaving the mountain. ..." It refers to these exalting events which took place before the disciples were again challenged to look at the cost of divine love.

Like the disciples, a week has passed for us and we are again reminded of the total commitment of Jesus. He is the serving, suffering man of God, totally faithful to God, even if that means death. God, in his turn, is totally faithful to his beloved Son in raising him from death.

How disappointing for Jesus that his followers worry and compete for positions of prestige and honor. "What were you arguing about on the road?" like "Who do you say I am?" is a proper question for any disciple, whether then or now, there or right here. What do we do with the gift of discipleship?

That is where the little child piece is so important. "Anyone who welcomes one of these little children in my name welcomes me." He makes himself as vulnerable as a little child. Cruelty to children, neglect, abuse of trust cuts us to the heart. How could such things happen? Yet Jesus puts himself there, at risk. He is within the little ones. He is also within the disciple. There he can be embraced and welcomed or neglected, betrayed, cruelly misrepresented. He, like the little child, is in our hands.

The only expression that Jesus makes here and now of his love, compassion forgiveness and of his teaching is through his disciples. He is in our hands in the same way as a little child is in the hands of adults. What becomes of Jesus or of little children, to a great extent depends on those who are supposed to love them.

The expression of the love of Jesus is revealed in the way love is shown to those with little power or support of their own: those who have nothing to give in return, except love. Our own experience of those who most express the teaching of Jesus is not of those who make friends in high places to promote their cause or show their prestige, but through those who make themselves one with the poor, the powerless, the little ones. Whom would you hold up as an example of Christian living to someone who had never heard of Jesus?

Twenty-sixth Sunday of Ordinary Time

"Jesus summoned the twelve and began to send them out in pairs giving them authority over the unclean spirits." (Mark 6:17) Yes, the twelve had the authority from Jesus. John, recalling this, objected to this outsider who was not "one of us." Throughout the Gospels until the very end, Jesus identifies himself with his disciples. He dwells in them, prays in them, heals and forgives in them. It is in them that he will go to the ends of the earth, preaching to every nation. But who are we to limit his activity or to decide who is "one of us." Time and again we experience the "cup of water" coming from unexpected hands. Jesus accepts the gift with loving gratitude and abundantly blesses the giver.

Being a bearer of the life and teaching of Jesus, as he has warned us over the last two weeks, has its hazards. The dangers of preaching a message and living a message of universal love and total forgiveness in a selfish world did not make Jesus cautious. He does not want his followers to shrivel up and die of caution. Today he warns his followers that God knows the hearts of all. What we are asked to do constantly is to look into our own hearts and let God work in whomever he wills. How truly are we living the message so that it is heard by the world? What has to go?

Modern surgery has given to thousands of people the option of choosing to sacrifice part of the body for the sake of keeping their lives. In fact it is an immense relief to be told, for example, that a cancer has gone no further and that surgery will cut out the threat to life. The process may be painful in more ways that one, but ultimately it is welcome.

Jesus speaks of spiritual surgery. It is the call to take drastic saving action. It may seem as drastic as the loss of eye or hand or foot. But it will prevent life being taken over and sapped away.

Have you ever met a person consumed with bitterness or hatred or the desire for revenge? Love and joy and spirit can be lost to consuming passion. Greed, ambition, sexual pleasure, can all drive out any consideration for the feelings of others. The addict is a sorry, lost person while ever the addiction persists.

While no one is beyond the healing power of Jesus, he pleads with us in graphic terms to cut out the evil before it has taken over life; before life is lost to it.

If any destructive attitude begins to surface, let it surface, then look at it, admit it, assess it. Perhaps to "tear it out" or "cut it off" will feel like loss. Here we may need the presence of Jesus in the disciple who may be trusted friend, professional helper, spiritual adviser, good confessor. Perhaps the cutting and then the healing will take time and involve suffering. It is the decision and the prayer that accompanies it that will enable Jesus to touch the wound and heal, to cast out this devil and make way for the fuller presence of God.

Or, we may be disciples called and empowered to act in the name of Jesus in this healing process for another. Attentive, compassionate listening is a powerful gift. The hope of Moses was, "If only the whole people of the Lord were prophets, and the Lord gave his Spirit to them all!" Through Christ this hope can be fulfilled.

Twenty-seventh Sunday of Ordinary Time

Today's liturgy offers the option of leaving out of the Gospel reading verses 13 to 16. These are about the little children. Some may think that this passage confuses the strong message about marriage.

It seems to me that it explains what has gone before. "Anyone who does not welcome the kingdom of God like a little child will never enter it." Openness, simplicity, trust, truth, frank communication, self acceptance, acceptance of others, freedom to ask for help or to express a need or a feeling are all qualities of an unsophisticated child. The child is not afraid to love or to be loved without pretence. Unfortunately as we grow we learn to conform, to hide the real because of some perceived unworthiness or in an attempt to please. Rejection, ridicule, unfair comparisons, forced competition and the call to succeed at all cost, kill the little child, ruin the reality that God has created and produce a caricature.

"The Lord said, 'It is not good to be alone.'" The child will not be alone because of the freedom and trust that simplicity sustains. One who has lost the child within is alone even in a crowd, because of the fear of being discovered.

God calls us out of destructive loneliness into creative relationships. Through trustful, trusting relationships the child can be reborn, life can come to fullness, God's presence is confirmed and expressed through his image in us.

It is no accident that marriage is a sacrament. A sacrament brings about God's supernatural presence or confirms that presence or empowers it for a special purpose. Surely marriage is this liberating, creative, life-giving force. God's gift is unity with himself. The freedom made possible by our human growth through the love of the other prepares a place for his grace.

The instrument of his saving power, his presence, his grace is in this case, not water or oil but the love, intimate relationship and commitment of human beings who can be totally free together. This freedom brought about and nourished by human love, trust and acceptance is the power that re-creates the child that may have been suppressed. Each is loved as he or she is. Each is challenged to become what God created in a climate of trust, love and care where both are free to say and to be the person they are. In such a relationship, as love increases, knowledge, experience and the passage of time nurture true wisdom.

The unfolding of the person, the discovery of the being God created each to be and the living of that reality are the designed results of marriage. This is the climate, too, in which children can grow in happiness, freedom and maturity.

What, then, of the person who is not married? What of me? "It is not good that the man should be alone." God says this to all men and women. We can not reach our potential without interaction with others. We all need intimacy. We all need those to whom we can trust ourselves. We all need to have a climate, a person, a community with whom we can be ourselves and say and be who we are with the security of true love. We all need those who can tell us the truth about ourselves and to whom we can speak truthfully without the fear of rejection or anger. Freedom and growth require trust and truth. True love does not fear to speak out in praise and in encouragement, to listen with openness, to point out apparent defects with tentative gentleness. Whatever is done will be understood to be done through love and for good. It is in this climate that a person will grow to be authentic everywhere and with everyone.

Discovery of self comes through real and loving relationships.

God becomes more and more obviously present in relationships of marriage or friendship that are lived in such a way as to help his people grow to the full knowledge of the wonder he has created. Those fortunate people who have become the little child of the kingdom have reached maturity.

Twenty-eighth Sunday of Ordinary Time

"What must I do to inherit eternal life?" The hymn for Evening Prayer of the Church for Holy Saturday begins:

> My God I love thee—though there were
> No heaven for me to win
> No hell to punish those who dare
> Against thy will to sin.

It closes with:

> The love that asks not anything
> Love like thy own love free,
> Jesus, I give, who art my king,
> Who art my God, to thee.

In his response to the young man, Jesus tells us that it is not only what we do that brings eternal life, but where our hearts are. He told us elsewhere, "Where your treasure is, there will your heart be also." (Luke 12:34)

What is the motivating force of the young man's life? Is it a love for God so real that it will drive out the fear of any risk?

The kingdom of heaven was the young man's goal. I wonder how he understood it. How do we understand it? We do not even know what following Jesus in his kingdom will imply or call us to be and do in life from day to day. We do know that it involves a relationship of love that will overcome fear of the loss of anything that diminishes that love. Its

completion in heaven is more incomprehensible still. These
are "things beyond the mind of man, all that God has prepared
for those who love him." (1Corinthians 2:9) This blessed state
has one thing in common with the journey. Its essence is love,
a love already established and confirmed along the way.

Jesus hit the spot when he got the young man to focus on
his wealth. Money and possessions are a great touchstone for
testing genuine commitment and the quality of relationships.
This is true of our relationship with God and of our relationships with others. Do we trust God enough to risk our goods,
money or future when conscience requires it, expressing a love
of whole heart and mind and soul?

God calls us to himself through relationships with others,
loving them as ourselves. How do these calls for genuine love
integrate with what is perceived to be mine or yours or ours?
Last week we reflected on the special relationships of marriage
and intimate friendship. Can we really say we commit ourselves in total mutual love and trust and then not trust each
other with what we own?

Consider the words of Brian Wicker from an article in the
English *Tablet*:

> I suspect that if it were made a condition of a
> Christian marriage that the couple had to pool
> all their money in a joint bank account, it
> would pull the couple up short with a real
> question: "Am I prepared to trust this other
> person with full access to all my money?" If the
> answer is no, the implication is clear: a proposed
> marriage should not go ahead, for a basic fea-
> ture of the sacrament is missing. ("Viewpoint,"
> 24.9.94)

No matter what our state in life, no matter by what roads
we travel to God in his kingdom here, we can never possess his
total presence in the final kingdom without returning, in our

finite way, the total love he has for us. Trust, generosity, unselfishness, letting go, are signs of this.

Some seem to have done this in an instant, like St Paul or St Francis of Assisi. But I wonder if they, too, had not already traveled a journey of struggle through the rough ways before the place was clear for God's pure light to penetrate.

We have begun the journey, thank God. We must say yes to his love to allow that love to touch us. The yes must be total somewhere along the way of life or after life. Praying for the dead makes sense as we encounter partial response to total love.

Twenty-ninth Sunday of Ordinary Time

From the time that James and John were called by Jesus from their fishing nets and from their work with their father Zebedee, they must have felt that gradually they were emerging as the future right hand men in the kingdom. If there could not be two right hand men, then they would share, one at the right, one at the left. To be at the top was important. Peter, however, would have represented a threat. If they were singled out at times, so was he. It was not just James and John, but Peter, James and John. Moreover he had never been one to stand back with his outspoken nature and forthright manner. Jesus had even given Peter a special name. He was no longer Simon the fisherman but Peter the rock.

The time had come for a little gentle lobbying. If they could stick together they had the numbers. The woman's vote would not do any harm. In his account of these events Matthew tells us that the mother of Zebedee's sons approached Jesus. (Matthew 20:20–21)

Zebedee's name appears more often in the Gospels than the names of some of the Apostles. The fact that his wife was at the cross with the faithful women and Mary is evidence that this family, not just the sons, were close to Jesus. It seemed that the boys had a great future ahead in the kingdom.

It was not till the end and the new beginning that James and John eventually learned how trivial all of this was. They would learn what it was to be at the side of Jesus. Here he asks the question, "Do you know what you are asking? Can you drink the cup?" Their answer, in unison, comes so quickly, so glibly, "We can." They don't stop to ask what he means by, "drink the cup."

James and John, together with any true follower of Jesus, will learn that position, power, talent, skill or authority in the kingdom are gifts for the service of others. Whatever work we do can be done as a gracious service, graciously done. Seats at the side of Jesus in his kingdom on earth are not comfortable seats from which his followers direct an obedient and sub-servient world. They are the trouble seats from which their occupants are called by a love that will not let them sit by idly while the selfish "make their authority felt" and inflict injustice on God's children. The cup of communion with Jesus incorporates us into the life of the Just One, the suffering servant of God.

God exercises his power through those who, like Jesus, unconcerned for their own prestige and comfort, empty themselves of pride to become his channel of life and love. These chosen ones become the servants of God's people, never ashamed to serve. "His state was divine, yet Christ Jesus did not cling to his equality with God, but emptied himself to assume the condition of a slave." (Philippians 2:6)

It is in unselfish service that we grow into the image of Jesus, image of the Father. "The Son of Man himself did not come to be served, but to serve and to give his life as a ransom for many."

Thirtieth Sunday of Ordinary Time

What was all the commotion? Why had the crowd gathered? Then, "he heard it was Jesus of Nazareth." Here was the once-in-a-lifetime chance, the golden opportunity that would never knock again. Bartimaeus could not see, but he could hear the good news and he could shout his response to it. As the poor, the powerless and those who are different from the crowd are put in their place, so was he scolded and told to keep quiet. But Jesus was on his way, moving away from Jericho, out of his life. This was no time for listening to cautious, well-established people. "He only shouted louder, 'Son of David, have pity on me.'"

Jesus passed through the crowd, surely passing others on the roadside, but for this one, he stopped. Bartimaeus had called from his heart to Jesus, now Jesus calls him. "Call him here" he said with an authority his followers do not question. It seems to free them from their inhibitions as they enter into the ministry of Jesus by not only calling the man but reassuring him. "'Courage,' they said, 'get up, he is calling you.'" They, too, are called from being scolders to being encouragers.

When the rich young man was called, excess baggage held him back, preventing him from moving. (Mark 10:17) In contrast here, we witness the leap of faith that leaves all impediments behind. There is significance in Mark's short sentence, "So throwing off his cloak, he jumped up and went to Jesus." The past was finished, except for the elements in it that would grow into the image of the one he was to see. An experience, a life, such as his wrapped in the new cloak of Jesus, would certainly clothe one with deep compassion.

"What do you want me to do for you?" Need had nurtured deep desire. He did not have to think twice about the answer. People who are more fortunate in life, when asked the same question, sometimes give the answer, "I don't really know what I want." Fed with so many things, they are starved of deep desire and childlike spontaneity. "Master let me see again" comes spontaneously from deep desire.

The wonder of the thing is that need has caused Bartimaeus to desire, and desire has led him to know his own poverty, which can be satisfied only by God through the Son of David, his fellow human being passing along the way dispensing the power of the all-powerful.

Bartimaeus was dismissed, "'Go, your faith has saved you.' And immediately his sight returned." But he did not go away or back, but forward. "He followed him along the road."

The once-in-a-lifetime, golden opportunity, had come his way. He grasped it. But now he saw with his eyes and with his heart, mind and faith-filled soul, that there was more here than sight to blind eyes. Where the road would lead, he did not know. But here before him was the true way to the God-given end of that road, wherever or whatever that was to be.

Thirty-first Sunday of Ordinary Time

Emotional and psychological maturity, health, satisfying relationships, self-acceptance and the acceptance of others, moral conduct and happiness itself, all depend on our acceptance of what is, and our response to that reality.

Some things we should try to change, some we should not; some things we are able to change, some we are not. This is true of each of us individually and of society.

Whatever the case, we must begin with reality. Is this the reality? Is it as it should be? Can I do something to make it as it should be? What is it I can do?

Jesus knew anxious people and counseled them not to worry about things over which they had no control. "Can any of you for all his worrying add a single cubit to his span of life?" (Luke 12:25)

On the other hand, many things are in our control. Here he told us to act boldly and decisively to eliminate things destructive to personal and social life. In graphic language he said, "If your hand should cause you to sin, cut it off." And in action, "He went into the Temple and began driving out those who were selling. 'According to the scripture,' he said, 'my house will be a house of prayer. But you have turned it into a robbers' den.'" (Luke 19:45–46)

What then is the basic fact, once known and accepted, upon which all others depend, from which all healthy, moral, loving thoughts and actions stem? "What is the first of all commandments?" It all depends on reality and on our response to reality. What is the basic reality?

Jesus tells us here. God is, and God is love absolute, love unconditional, love universal. The only authentic response to this absolute Love who has willed my being out of love and for love, is itself love. The answer of Jesus to the question of the fundamental rule of life is precisely that. "You must love the Lord your God with all your heart, with all your soul, with all your mind and with all your strength."

The mind comprehends, in part, the wonder; the heart responds in love; the soul is opened to the flood of grace; and all our strength is directed by the will to express this immense love in our lives.

The second great reality is that every other human being is, as I am, the result of God's creative love. Each is loved by God as his child. Possessing his love, sharing his being, I am a reflection of his love for all. This is the reality. Morality, truth, happiness is knowing this reality and responding to it by living it. Being what I am is the basis of happiness. I am made in God's image. That is the image of loving Creator.

From time to time we have to ask, "In these specific circumstances, what is the most loving thing I can do or say?" The answer is not always obvious. We may need the advice of others in discerning complex issues. But if we honestly search, using facts, listening to advice and having the attitude of the compassionate Jesus, we will always act lovingly. At times we will make mistakes in our choices of action. In these cases we accept the fact of our human frailty, try to amend the situation and, we hope, become more loving and wiser by the experience. In any case, in the words of the hymn—"Where there is charity and love, there the love of God abides."

Thirty–second Sunday of Ordinary Time

About this time of the year we celebrate the Feast of all the Saints. In today's Gospel story Jesus draws attention to what a saint is. The widow who lets go of her last two coins gave all she had in order to give glory to God. In this she is the image of Jesus who gave all. That is what a saint is.

Jesus is the perfect image of his Father. We, too, are made in God's image and are one with Jesus through baptism. We are confirmed in his Spirit and continually united with him in the Eucharist. Living this all-giving life of Jesus is holiness.

If we were able to compare the life of this otherwise unknown woman with the life of Jesus—what they both looked like, what they said, did or accomplished, the way they died, the memory they left behind—they would probably seem to have nothing in common. But sameness is not the image and likeness we are called to be. Each person is different, individual. We are called to live our own individual lives. The similarity is the spirit in which we live and by which we are motivated. The gift is being who we are and living that in total gift to God. It is a loving response to the gifts he has bestowed on us.

The canonized saints themselves display an immense variety in the way life is lived for God and for others. The motivating spirit, the total love and the longing for God are the same.

"Many of the rich people put in a great deal." It is true that many rich people put a great deal into achieving results. Performance, results, profit, acceptance because of position, position because of money, money because of performance. So the cycle goes around and around, sometimes without the time to stop and ask the important questions. It is safer to buy power and security than to respect the freedom of others and to trust God. It is safer to hang back than to risk helping and risk being rejected or hurt. It is safer not to volunteer in case more is asked. It is safer to give less than what is possible in case something crops up. It is safer not to let people know they are loved and valued in case they make use of the information. While all this is taking place we are living, but only partly living, because the spontaneous, child-like spirit of Jesus is given little room to grow and draw us into full trust of Our Father.

If we give only what is left over and will never be missed, we need to ask for the spirit of Jesus. His last gift was the breath of his liberating spirit as he committed his life into God's hands. "Father into your hands I commit my spirit," (Luke 23:46) was the dying prayer of one whose whole life was lived in the hands of his loving Father in total trust.

Following God's way may seem risky at times. Doing the ethical, moral, truthful, honest, generous, loving thing may seem foolish.

The first lesson, as does the Gospel, offers an example of such risk and foolishness. The woman has a few sticks, a handful of meal and a little oil. But she really hears the words of Elijah, "Do not be afraid," as God's words, and is fool enough to believe and give all she has. God saw her through.

What a destructive thing is fear. What a liberating thing is trust.

Thirty-third Sunday of Ordinary Time

"Heaven and earth will pass away, but my words will not pass away."

The words of Jesus that will never pass away, even in eternity, he has summarized in the two great commandments. In these two are contained everything Jesus had to say about our response to our loving God and to his creation. He guarantees, "Do this and life is yours." (Luke 10:28) and "On these two commandments hang the whole law and the prophets also." (Matthew 22:40)

"You must love the Lord your God with all your heart, with all your soul, with all your mind ... you must love your neighbor as yourself," will never pass away. In heaven there will be no faith, hope, theology, sacraments, earth, sea or sky. Love will remain. The loving relationships established here between us and God and with each other will come to perfection.

In the meantime we keep creating our own images of heaven and earth. They keep passing away. Each time one of our creations passes away there is confusion, pain, anger, distress and sorrow. It is as though the sun has been darkened, the moon lost its brightness, the stars are tumbling about us. Our heaven and earth are shaken to the foundations. People lose heart.

The followers of Jesus experienced this in the first century. They waited in vain for the end of the world and for the second coming of Jesus. He had said, "Before this generation has passed away all these things will have taken place." In their confusion they had to cling to his words, the essential words, and to discover another meaning to this apocalyptic language. As one false heaven and earth passed away, a wider vision of heaven and earth and the kingdom was enabled, after confusion.

These disturbing experiences continued. Centuries later Galileo exposed a false image of heaven and earth. Again, after confusion, pain and turmoil, deeper insights were gained. The discovery of the "New World" brought the heavens and earth of many tumbling about them. Were these newly discovered people human and if so what of redemption for them? The Reformation, the Enlightenment, archeological and paleontological discoveries, physical and psychological insights into human makeup, new insights into the Bible, all brought their measure of turmoil. Little or large heavens and earths were crashing down. But each further discovery, each truth revealed, eventually led to a deeper appreciation of the real heaven and the real earth—God's creation, not ours.

In our own times the Second Vatican Council was deliberately designed to open windows onto the truth of the Church in the modern world. Again, people felt they had lost some essential element in their picture of heaven and earth. Again, as things came tumbling down, the view of the real and essential was clearer. The words of Jesus have not, and will never, pass away.

Images of the Church and the world may change. The essential of God's word through Jesus will only grow clearer out of all our confusion if we continue to seek the truth with love, and to love with truth.

The Feast of Christ the King

Jesus contrasts the two kingdoms: the kingdom of this world and "My kingdom." The immediate point of identity of the first is the power of force. "If my kingdom were of this world, my men would have fought. ... Truth is the mark of identity for my kingdom," the kingdom of God.

Remember that Jesus told us that, "the kingdom of God is within you." (Luke 17:21) Which kingdom is within us? "Us" as individuals, family, household, community, parish, nation, Church?

Often we address God as "all powerful." Power is a holy thing, it is of God. Reflection on the way God exercises his power will help. God creates, giving his creatures force and direction, giving human beings the power to love and to choose, the power to participate in his creative, loving power. Even though we abuse this power and turn it to destruction and hatred, he never uses force to restrict it. When James and John asked Jesus to let them "call down fire from heaven to burn them up" (the inhospitable Samaritans), Jesus "rebuked them." (Luke 9:54–55) When his followers asked, "Lord shall we use our swords" (to defend Jesus by force) (Luke 22:49), the rebuke is consistent with his reply to Pilate in today's Gospel. His trust is not in force, but in truth and in the God of truth and love.

Is this, then, the King who reigns in our hearts, homes, community, parish, nation, Church?

We can only speculate as to the kind of world and Church we would have if all the followers of Jesus had taken him seriously.

We can, however, do more than speculate about our present response to his call to belong to a kingdom not of this world. Each of us can ask whether our use of power is destructive or creative, whether it inhibits true freedom in others or encourage their freedom, whether it limits our own true freedom or liberates us.

Our response to these questions may be, "I have no power." Anyone who can understand these words and even some who can not, do have power.

How do we resolve problems and come to decisions? The Spirit of the kingdom of God would lead us to seek what is true and best—whether this be to our immediate advantage or not—through peaceful discussion, negotiation and sharing of ideas in a climate of respect for the needs of all and with prayerful trust in God. The kingdom of the world would urge the use of force and whatever power we may possess to gain our own advantage, to win. The force and power used either by individuals or by groups may be physical force, authority, shouting, temper, ridicule, silent sulking, unjust denial of needs or rights, abuse, whether physical, verbal or mental.

Any person or group is capable of abusing the God-given gifts of body or mind to obtain advantage. Any person is capable of responding to God's gifts by working for goodness, justice and peace through the quest for truth while trusting God.

The persons and groups in whose midst is the kingdom of God ask in every critical circumstance, what is true, what is best, what is creative, what would be false or destructive; what gives fuller life and freedom, what takes life or enslaves? All power and authority, if of the kingdom of God, is for service.

> Peace is more than the absence of war: it cannot
> be reduced to the maintenance of a balance of
> power between opposing forces, not does it
> arise out of despotic domination, but it is appro-
> priately called the "effect of righteousness".
> (Isaiah 32:17) It is the fruit of that right
> ordering of things with which the divine
> founder has invested human society. ...

These words from the Second Vatican Council's Decree on the
Church in the Modern World can be applied to us as individuals, families, households, communities, nations and Churches
as we seek the kingdom of justice, love and peace.